D0895768

GREEN
WITCHCRAFT III
THE MANUAL

Magic Sticks and Fairy Gifts: Creating a Wand

The Green Witch uses objects from nature for spell-work, magical teas, healing, and folkcrafts. For example, there is no need to spend a lot of money on a wand—nature offers them free of charge.

A wand is a tool used to direct energy. Wands may be selected from a variety of woods. Oak is typically viewed as a God-power wand, while willow is seen as Goddess-powered. If you want to focus on fairy magics, the wand could be elder or hawthorn.

The wand should measure the length of your forearm (from crook of the arm to the tip of your forefinger). To cut one for your use, the rule is: to get a gift, you must give a gift. Whenever you take something from Nature, you must give something back, both to express appreciation for the item and to offer compensation.

The gift you give may be the pouring of milk upon the roots of the tree, or the scattering of flower petals, or simply stating your appreciation and offering your blessing to the tree.

If you come across a stick that appears energized, it could be a fairy gift to you, and you may use that for your wand. Be sure to leave something in the place where you found the stick.

About the Author

Ann Moura (Aoumiel) has been a solitary practitioner of Green Witchcraft for over thirty-five years. She derived her Craft name, Aoumiel, to reflect her personal view of the balance of the male and female aspects of the Divine. Her mother and grandmother were Craftwise Brazilians of Celtic-Iberian descent who, while operating within a general framework of Catholicism, passed along a heritage of folk magic and Craft concepts that involved spiritism, ancient Celtic deities, herbal spells, Green magic, reincarnation belief, and rules for using "The Power."

The Craft was approached casually in her childhood, being experienced or used as situations arose. With the concepts of candle spells, herbal relationships to magic, spiritism, reincarnation, Rules of Conduct, and calling upon the Elementals and the Divine already established through her mother's teachings in particular, she was ready to proceed in her own direction with the Craft by the time she was fifteen. In her practice of the Craft today, Aoumiel has moved away from the Christianized associations used by her mother and grandmother. She is focused on the basic Green level of Witchcraft and is teaching the next generation in her family. She took both her Bachelor of Arts and Master of Arts degrees in history. She is married, has a daughter and a son, and is a certified history teacher at the high school level.

To Write to the Author

If you wish to contact the author or would like more information about this book, please write to the author in care of Llewellyn Worldwide and we will forward your request. Both the author and publisher appreciate hearing from you and learning of your enjoyment of this book. Llewellyn Worldwide cannot guarantee that every letter written to the author will be answered, but all will be forwarded. Please write to:

Ann Moura (Aoumiel)
% Llewellyn Worldwide
P.O. Box 64383, Dept. K688-2
St. Paul, MN 55164-0383, U.S.A.

Please include a self-addressed, stamped envelope with your letter.
If outside the U.S.A., enclose international postal coupons.

GREEN WITCHCRAFT III

THE MANUAL

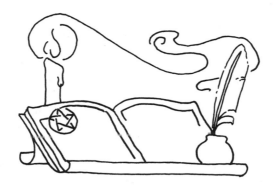

ANN MOURA

(AOUMIEL)

2000
Llewellyn Publications
St. Paul, Minnesota 55164-0383, U.S.A.

Green Witchcraft III: The Manual © 2000 by Ann Moura. All rights reserved. No part of this book may be used or reproduced in any manner whatsoever, including Internet usage, without written permission from Llewellyn Publications, except in the case of brief quotations embodied in critical articles or reviews.

FIRST EDITION
Second Printing, 2000

Cover design by Lisa Novak
Cover photo from Digital Stock
Interior illustrations by Carrie Westfall
Editing and design by Connie Hill
Based on original interior design by Rebecca Zins

Library of Congress Cataloging-in-Publication Data
Moura, Ann
     Green witchcraft III: the manual / Ann Moura
    (Aoumiel) — 1st ed.
      p.   cm. —
     Includes bibliographical references (p. 231) and index.
     ISBN 1–56718–688–2 (pbk)
   1. Witchcraft. 2. Herbs—Miscellanea. 3. Magic. 4. Ann Moura (Aoumiel) I. Title. II. Green Witchcraft: Folk Magic, Fairy Lore & Herb Craft   III. Green Witchcraft II: Balancing Light and Shadow.
BF1572.P43A58   2000
133.4'3—dc21   96-16406
                                                 CIP

Llewellyn Worldwide does not participate in, endorse, or have any authority or responsibility concerning private business transactions between our authors and the public. All mail addressed to the author is forwarded but the publisher cannot, unless specifically instructed by the author, give out an address or phone number.

Llewellyn Publications
A Division of Llewellyn Worldwide, Ltd.
P.O. Box 64383, Dept. K688-2
St. Paul, Minnesota 55164-0383, U.S.A.
www.llewellyn.com

 Printed in the United States of America

This book is dedicated, with love and blessings,
to the students and seekers of
the Green Path of Witchcraft

Other Books by Ann Moura

Dancing Shadows: The Roots of Western Religious Beliefs (as Aoumiel)

Green Witchcraft: Folk Magic, Fairy Lore & Herb Craft

Green Witchcraft II: Balancing Light and Shadow

Contents

Acknowledgements

My thanks and appreciation to those who have offered me their support and encouragement in teaching and writing about the Craft, and especially to my husband and children.

Special thanks to Nancy Mostad, Cynthia Ahlquist, Connie Hill, Becky Zins, D. J. Conway, and Jack Green for their help, suggestions, and good vibes. A big thank you goes to Light Hunter for his assistance in planning the illustrations. And although her poetry is not used in this book, I wish to acknowledge the darkly beautiful and moving poetry of Ril Kyannon, for the inspiration her work gives to me.

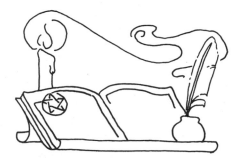

Introduction

This book is intended to be used in conjunction with my first book on the Craft, *Green Witchcraft: Folk Magic, Fairy Lore & Herb Craft*, with my second book, *Green Witchcraft II: Balancing Light and Shadow* as a supplemental text. Both books are referenced throughout this handbook, but the first book is the textbook for this course of study. My maternal heritage is Celtic Iberian, and it is through this lineage that my Craft descended to me. The Green Craft is what I learned from my Brazilian mother and grandmother as I grew up, and my personal studies in over thirty-five years of Solitary practice. The handbook you hold is based upon the classes I teach periodically at a local shop. With this book as your guide, you may take a student approach to learning the Green Craft as I have taught it to others.

Many of my students have found my first book, *Dancing Shadows* (Llewellyn, 1994) helpful for historical background. History is the field of study I enjoy and in which I hold both Bachelor and Master of Arts degrees. Through this study I can show students that Craft practices are grounded in real-time human history rather than in mythology or the romantic notions of any given era. Witchcraft is not something that sprang up in the

1940s and 1960s, with new Traditions appearing every decade since, but has been an ongoing part of our culture for many millennia. It is only in recent decades that the Craft has gone public. That the Old Religion is being revived and brought out into society for others to learn of is a matter of great joy to me. I cannot praise enough the writers who bring to the public the traditions of their particular cultural background. By reading about a variety of practices, students can select those aspects that appeal to them and set aside the ones that do not.

My course consists of eight classes, representative of the eight Sabbats of witchcraft. There is a lot of information in each class, so I recommend you spread out your studies, practice the lessons, and work on the projects at your own pace.

Try to follow the course as a regular class would progress. Use a notebook, *Green Witchcraft* as your basic textbook (and this will be referred to in the Manual as the textbook or the text), and do the assignments and projects of each chapter just as would be expected of a student in a classroom situation. *Green Witchcraft II* includes topics such as meditations, stones and crystals, and the ogham, while focusing on the balanced use of the dark powers in magic. The final exam will reflect how comfortable you feel with the practice of magic and the presence of the ancient powers of the earth and the universe. Bright blessings to you as you explore the Green path.

—Ann Moura (Aoumiel)

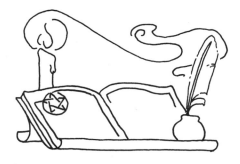

Class 1
Introduction to the Craft;
Basic Equipment &
Altar/Working Area

Introduction

Witchcraft

Witchcraft is legally recognized as the religion called Wicca. It is basically a revival of the pre-Christian view of the universe and our place in it as intrinsic partners with Nature. There are a number of shamanic concepts in this *Old Religion*, including the ability of the individual to commune directly with Nature, blend with other life forces, and travel to other realms, planes of existence, worlds, and universes. The Craft, as witchcraft and the Old Religion are also called, holds a holistic view of the world in which a person is related to all life through the flow of universal energy.

Knowledge and science are embraced by witches as gifts of the Divine that they can use to advance spiritually while following their own life path. The pantheons of pre-Christian societies are often used as the foundation for modern Craft denominations, or "Traditions," identifying with Egyptian,

1

Norse, Celtic, Greek, Roman, Indian, Middle Eastern, or African deities. Some Traditions are called eclectic and work with deities picked from various pantheons.

Since the 1940s there has been a revival of many of the old beliefs, including the duality of the Divine as a Goddess and a God, the power of the Elementals, and the ability to create changes through magical practice. Several Traditions of witchcraft have been around since the 1960s, and are denominations, as it were, of the Craft. Many of these Traditions have adopted standardized rules and procedures, passing these on to their membership in coven (assembly) settings. The coven may be very small or very large, but usually larger covens branch off into smaller ones so that group work involving the raising of energy can be better controlled and directed. The preferred number of members in a complete coven is thirteen, but, in reality, that varies quite a lot. For a review of the different types of Wiccan groups and their approaches to the Craft, I recommend Margot Adler's book, *Drawing Down the Moon* (Beacon Press, 1979).

Many of the key issues of social interaction are guided by the generally accepted rules of most covens. The Witches' Rede is the guiding rule of: "If it harms none, do what you will." With this as the basic tenet of the practice of the Craft, everything else is a matter of selecting what actually works best for you. This principle is used to determine what changes a witch wants to make, and how to go about achieving a desired result. In family heritage and for solitary witches, there is less need for the dogma common to groups. Some covens levy monetary fines for even minor infractions of coven rules. For some witches this may detract from the sense of independence and freedom associated with the Craft, and inhibit personal spiritual growth. The coven setting is not for everyone, and most practicing witches are in fact solitaries who may or may not gather with other witches for special high-energy observations such as the Esbats and the Sabbats.

The rituals of the Sabbats and the Esbats are expressions of unity with the earth, the moon, and the universe in the harmonious flow of life-energy. During these holy days of observance, the witch reaffirms union with what in the Green Craft is often simply called *The Power.* There are various mythologies to express the eight Sabbats (some can be found on pages 25–28 of the textbook), but for now, we will focus on the practice of Green Witchcraft.

Green Witchcraft: 3 Styles of Practice

Welcome to Green Witchcraft. A lot of people wonder what kind of witchcraft is called green. Some people have heard of white witchcraft and black witchcraft, and even gray witchcraft, but green is sometimes surprising. In my experience, there really is no such thing as black, white, or gray witchcraft, so that narrows the field a bit. Let me explain. The concept of black and white, with gray presumably somewhere in between, comes from the polarization of modern social thinking. By modern, I mean the past 2,000 to 3,000 years. People have been around for a long time, as proven by 300,000-year-old cave paintings and 400,000-year-old spears. Many people are still attuned to the earth and nature, practicing spiritually connective rites with balance, not dichotomy. Dichotomy is a feature of modern, not ancient, western society and culture, wherein black equates to evil and white equates to good. Gray, then, becomes a mixture of good and evil, composing a kind of ambiguous spiritual soup. None of that is part of the Craft as I was taught it by my mother and her mother—they taught balance and interconnection.

So what exactly *is* Green Witchcraft? It is the core practice of the traditions of earth magics, the Witchcraft of the Natural Witch, the Kitchen Witch, the Cottage Witch, the Hedge Witch. It is herbal, attuned to nature, and basic in the sense that it is the foundation upon which any Craft tradition may be built. In the three-leveled triangle pattern of Northern European tradition, the word "green" is used to describe the ground level belonging to the ancient Goddess and God of Nature. I find this very appropriate, since the deities of the upper levels are essentially the newer social ones relating to class distinctions (warrior: Thor, priesthood/lawgiver: Tyr, and ruler: Odin).

The green level of practice addresses the God and the Goddess as the powerful forces of Nature. This is the magics of the people as social equals, which was the Old Religion held by people in a communal time. As a ruler class developed, supported by a new class of lawmakers and enforced by a warrior class, each of these new social stratas were given their special representative deities and set off as higher levels upon the original green base.

In the Northern tradition, Frey and Freya were the deities of the common folk. These names translate as "Lord" and "Lady," and can be found in ancient religions using words with the same or similar meaning. The pre-Moslem Middle East had Allah and Allat, pre-Judaic Palestine had Yahweh and Asherat, and pre-Vedic India had (and still has) Shiva and Shakti. In each place, the imposition of a single dominant male deity at the pinnacle of the divine pantheons resulted from priesthoods formalizing a dogma that supported a social structure of divine-sanctioned rulership.

Yahweh, God (in Christianity), Allah, and in India, Brahma took over the lead roles, but were basically unapproachable, so intercession took place through the priesthood, and saints generated from and ordained by the priesthood. This had the effect of taking power from the general population, of isolating the people from their deities, and empowering a ruler supported by religious authority and a standing army that formed a warrior class.

Today, much of that social system has faded away, and thus we see a struggle over redefining the role of religion and government in the social order. Civil law has gained the power of the ruler, and a priesthood is no longer required to support the civil law. One of the major sources of unrest in many lands today comes from the tension between those who want ethical laws and those who want to impose what they perceive as "God's law."

The practice of the green level of the Craft draws the powers of Nature into the individual to create changes through magical workings. The Power is not some distant, amorphous thing, but real energy and the flow of that energy to develop your own self-empowerment. The more the energy is used, the easier it flows.

The Green practice is not formal, but utilizes herbs in spell-work, magical teas, healing, and folkcrafts. Using the objects in nature, the Green Witch is able to construct spells with what materials are on hand. And these spells, charms, and other magics work through the Elementals, who are the four basic Powers of Witchcraft: Earth, Air, Fire, and Water. The Elementals will be covered more in depth in another class.

When I first started teaching this course, it was very generic because I was addressing mainly newcomers to the Craft, or those who were only mildly curious about it. They were unaware of the potency of The Power so my approach was more cautious. My mother and grandmother referred to *The Power,* but I see this as the Goddess and the God, and the Elementals. To me, the Green Craft is very natural, practical, grounded, and earth centered. The energy flow is *real,* and it is *divine.*

After teaching a couple of basic courses in witchcraft, I was dissatisfied that some of my students "got it" and others just sort of dabbled. That was when I changed my program of instruction. What is in this handbook is the "hands-on" course that I now offer for serious students only. If you are not sure that you want to invoke the Ancient Powers of the earth and the universe, then put this book back on the shelf. If you are ready for a new life, one that opens to you the doors between the worlds, and puts you in direct contact with The Power, then keep reading. I have had students tell me about the transformations that have taken place in their lives, and this offers me encouragement to keep teaching. It is my hope that you, the reading student, will experience a magical transformation as well.

In the Green Craft, there are three basic styles of practice. This does not mean that one style is better than another, or more effective than another, or a "level" of development. It does mean that you can chose how you want to practice the Craft so that you are comfortable with magic and the contact you will have with the power and forces of Nature.

The first style of Craft practice exists within a mainstream religious affiliation. This is the practice of folk magics using the imagery of the divine as found in the mainstream religion of choice. For Catholics, in particular, this is an easy transition simply because so much of Catholicism is based upon pagan precedents. The goddess image may be found in Mary, Mother of God; the god image is in Jesus. The various saints, real people or former deities, may be used in folk magics to represent aspects of pagan deities: Saint Francis as the Lord of Animals; Saint Bridget was first the goddess Brigid ("The High One"). Many of the early saints of Catholicism were not *real* people, but pagan deities humanized, converted to Christianity, and turned into saints by new myths. The cathedrals of Europe were built on top of the temples and holy sites of various pagan deities. Pagan holy shrines and sacred wells were rededicated to Christian saints or to the ancient gods and goddesses redefined as saints (as with England's Chalice Well once being Brigid's). The pagan energies may still be called upon, but with modern names.

The second style of practice involves working directly with the natural powers without any religious figures or outlook. Similar to Elementalism, but without worship, the energies of Earth, Air, Fire, and Water are addressed. With this second style of Green Witchcraft, the practitioner is drawing the power inside to channel toward his or her goal. Various objects and items from Nature can be used to aid in focusing the energy, including such things as leaves, seed pods, feathers, stones, herbs, and shells.

The third style of Green Witchcraft brings the practitioner into close connection with the Goddess and the God, and the Elementals. This is both magic and religion. You can address the Divine and may eventually want to make a personal commitment to the Lady and the Lord. Once the channel is opened between you and them, particularly after a Dedication Ritual, the conversation is on-going—there is no "amen," no "thank you and good-bye." They personally give you a new name, called a "Working Name," to be kept secret between you and them. Because of the intensity of the connection between the practitioner and the Divine, I caution people not to do a Dedication (text pages 152–158) unless they are absolutely certain that a new way of life is what they desire. If you perform the Dedication and are just messing around ("Gosh, will it *really* work?"), you risk insulting The Power, and possibly ending your ability to connect with the Divine of the Craft in this life. Should they be inclined to give you a second chance, they may set many obstacles in your path and test you severely before you are rewarded with the open communication that comes from the Dedication.

If you want to practice the Craft, but want to remain within the socially accepted fold of mainstream religion, the first style is for you. If you want to forget about "religion" and simply be one with Nature, the second style is for you. If you feel that spiritual fulfillment will only come to you by connection with the Divine, along with being one with Nature, then the third style may be what you are looking for. I have used all three approaches successfully, so I know all three work. It is a matter of what is comfortable for you.

Rules of Conduct

The practice of the Green Craft has very basic rules. My mother repeated these rules of conduct over and over to me. Because I was showing the points of similarity between the rules and the Witches' Rede, I have presented the Rules of Conduct in the textbook (pages 76 and 78) in an order slightly different from how my mother taught them to me. Here is how my mother intoned the five rules to me (text page 143):

- Be careful what you do

- Be careful who you trust

- Do not use The Power to hurt another because what is sent comes back

- Never use The Power against someone else who has The Power

- To use The Power you must feel it in your heart and know it in your mind

The first rule is a warning to think through any spell or magical working so that it works as intended, and does not impinge on another person's freedom and individuality. There are times when it is tempting to help someone, but unless you have that person's consent, you ought not to work magic for their benefit. There are exceptions, of course. When you sense someone is endangered, it is natural to try to assist, but for the working to be optimally effective, that person should consent or ask for your aid.

However, where there is a matter of life or death, and the person is not available for comment, it becomes a personal judgment call. My mother and I worked our candle magics very hard to ensure my brother returned safely from Vietnam when we both felt there was life-threatening danger for him in his departure from that land (mentioned on page 83 of the text). What I left out in that telling was that when he raced through a field to catch the helicopter out of the country, he stepped on a land mine called a "Bouncing Betty." This type of land mine springs up into the air when triggered, and explodes at about knee level. The Bouncing Betty claimed the legs and/or the lives of many soldiers. My brother told us later that he felt the thing underfoot, saw it spring up at him, and could not believe it when the mine did not explode. He continued running to the helicopter, under fire. The helicopter was shot down, he had to transfer to another, and that one, too, was shot down. It took "three" helicopters to get him out of there, but he made it home safely, and has never indicated that he would have preferred it any other way. Our energies worked together.

You may not want to interfere with someone's karmic balance by eliminating a test they need to go through to aid in their spiritual growth, yet you ought to be able to determine when your help is right. Hence, "Be careful what you do."

I feel that the admonition of "Be careful who you trust" has its roots in the persecutions of the practitioners of the old ways. Many of the craftwise were forced underground, and thus they needed to be careful about who knew of their magical workings. Yet even today, if you are not "out of the broom closet" there will be people you may not want to confide in because they will talk it up around the workplace, neighborhood, or whatever. Sometimes, too, the very people who appear to be open-minded or sympathetic to the old ways turn out to be very conservative or narrow in their acceptance of witchcraft. Judgment comes in again, then, and the rule still has value.

Do not let others use this rule against you, either—such as asking you to reveal your working name. See text pages 39–40 about the various types of names. The Craft Name may double as the working name if no one else knows your Craft name, but after a dedication ritual the new name you receive from the Lady and the Lord defines you and is your Working Name. The Craft name that is used in the presence of others of like mind should not be used as your working name, so when you do spells, and other magics, if you have not done the Dedication Ritual, create your own second name to be your working name and keep it secret. The secrecy adds to the energizing power of your magics.

"Do not use The Power to hurt another because what is sent comes back," is a warning that the energies you call upon travel full circle. It is also a caution to you to look to alternate ways of dealing with the problems that come up in day-to-day living. The Power is not to be used frivolously to get back at someone who has said or done something that offends you. Doing so may afford a moment of smug revenge, but the energy released will draw like energy to you.

"Never use The Power against someone else who has The Power," for you both draw from the same well. My mother saw this as an expression of kinship between the people who had The Power. For her, family was all, and this is a Celtic tradition. The ties of kinship are of blood. For the witch, the ties of kinship are of spirit. We who practice are kin—brothers and sisters—and no matter how we interact on a personal basis, we are still kin. Kin does not harm kin. I have mentioned an episode in the textbook wherein a student once tried to create an issue between me and a sister, but instead of listening to her, we confided in each other and determined our mutual course of action, namely to cease her instruction until such time as she was emotionally ready. You must respect other practitioners of the Craft as you respect the Craft.

The Power is something that has to be "kenned." This is a kind of knowing that is all-encompassing, yet can be very subtle. When you ken something, you feel it is so. There is no doubt, and you do not entertain notions to the contrary of what is kenned. The Power is like that. Therefore, "to use The Power you must feel it in your heart and know it in your mind." You know that something will happen, and accept that. The sensation that goes with this is something that, once it is felt, will always be recognized. When there is the connection with the Divine and the Elementals, the feeling of The Power is very frequent and uplifting.

Tabbing the Textbook

To make the textbook, *Green Witchcraft: Folk Magic, Fairy Lore, and Herb Craft*, a useful tool, I recommend tabbing key pages for easy reference. Small or medium-sized clear or colored plastic tabs with label inserts can be bought in most office supply stores, discount stores, and even grocery stores in the school supplies section. The twenty tabs I suggest here are for this course, but you may want to tab other sections as well. Set your tabs into place before you remove the paper from the sticky film side. Be sure you have them arranged as you want them to look, spread out down the length of the book, so they are easy to see.

Page 51   Herbs   Page 169   Full Moon Esbat

Page 59   Incense/Trees   Page 177   New Moon Esbat

Page 63   Colors   Page 183   Yule

Page 67   Days and Hours   Page 193   Imbolc

Page 103   Runes   Page 203   Ostara

Page 105   Symbols   Page 211   Beltane

Page 123   Tarot   Page 219   Litha

Page 143   Rules and Sabbats   Page 229   Lughnassadh

Page 145   Basic Ceremony   Page 239   Mabon

Page 157   Cakes and Wine   Page 247   Samhain

As you work through this course, you will be utilizing the text as both a reference and a kind of menu. In putting together spells and charms, you will be selecting herbs, incenses, and colors, making inscriptions with the runes or other designs, conducting the work on an appropriate day and hour, and checking for symbols afterword to interpret what kind of response to expect.

Basic Equipment

Broom to Sweep Clear the Circle

There are some tools basic to the Craft, but these do not have to be very elaborate, cost a lot of money, or draw a lot of attention to you if discretion is what you prefer. The broom is one of the

easiest items to obtain. It is called a besom and is used to symbolically sweep clear the circle or sacred space prior to a ceremony or
ritual. The besom can be a traditional "witch's" broom such as

**The witch's familiar walks past her stang and besoms. The stang
may be either two or three-pronged, and may be decorated with a
wreath or other object appropriate to a sabbat.**

found in variety stores around Halloween. There are also the decorative type of brooms of various sizes sold in gift, hobby/craft, and flower shops. Usually the broom is plain, intended to be accented with dried flowers and ribbons, to be hung on a wall or on a door. This is fine for a besom. I do not recommend the kitchen broom, which will have about it the dust and household energies that may tend to interfere with your magical purpose. Even the "kitchen witch" (a witch who utilizes the objects of the everyday environment as magical tools—a rather homey practice of the Craft), usually also has a special broom for ritual.

Nature also offers plenty of brooms. You can use for a broom a fallen leafy branch, a fair-sized sprig of herb, or a shrubby twig. When out of doors, in particular, the fallen wood of trees provides a ready besom for ritual. I used to live in the Pacific Northwest and loved to use pine twigs to clear an area. To use such an item, simply acknowledge that it is perfect for your besom, sweep the area of the ritual, and offer your blessings to the energies of the woods (or wherever you are) for assisting you in your ritual. Then when you go, leave the sprig behind, usually in a decorative or artistic natural arrangement to show your appreciation—do not just toss it aside, but treat it with the respect due a ritual tool.

Ritual Knife

The ritual knife, the athame (pronounced: a-thau'may or a'tha-may), is one used to draw energy into your working, to create the circle, and to perform magical ceremonies. It is not a cutting tool, nor is it used to create the objects used in spellwork. The exception to this is in kitchen witchery. I have used a favorite paring knife for cookery magics, such as inscribing buns with the solar cross or chopping nuts for fruitcake when these are ritual foods for holidays. That knife exudes a special energy whenever I hold it, yet it is a kitchen tool.

The athame should be three-edged, that is double-sided and with a sharp point. A letter opener makes a perfect and inconspicuous ritual knife. For people who are in a situation where they have to be careful not to let others know of their interest in the Craft, the tools with the most ordinary appearance are the best.

There are also a number of occult or New Age shops that carry very attractive athames with various price tags, depending on how fancy the item. Athames may be made of crystals and silver, inlaid with gems, or they may be plain knives. Generally, a black handle is used for the athame as this color is protective, wards negativity, and draws power.

Wand

A wand is a tool used to direct energy and to energize objects. It is also used to greet and farewell the Elementals. Indeed, in typical pictures of witches, the magic wand is most often seen rather than the knife. The touch of the wand releases gathered energies into what is touched, and sets the magic to working. You could well practice without the athame and only have the wand. It is all a matter of preference and availability.

There is no need to spend a lot of money on a wand—Nature offers them free of charge. Wands may be selected from a variety of woods. I have several and use whichever one is appropriate to the working involved. Oak is typically sensed as a God-power wand, while willow is seen as Goddess-powered. There are any number of connections you can make between the wood used and the energy association. On page 59 of the text is a listing of woods and their qualities. On the next page are further associations with trees. If you want a wand symbolic of the balance of the Lady and the Lord working together, then you would want to use hazel wood. Indeed, hazel is considered the witch's tree because the witch recognizes the power as a duality in union.

If you want to focus on Fairy (or Faerie) magics, the wand could be alder or hawthorn. For the power of the Crone, use the elder. If you are unsure about what these trees look like, a quick look in an encyclopedia (under "Trees") will show some examples. There are also library books available on trees that can show you the various types and help you to recognize them.

The wand should measure the length of your forearm (from the crook of the arm to the tip of the forefinger). To cut one for your use, the rule is: *to get a gift, you must give a gift.* This is something that my mother and grandmother followed with great care. Whenever you take something from Nature, you must give something back. There is a two-fold purpose to this. The first reason is to express appreciation for the item. The second is to offer compensation. The gift you give may be the pouring of milk upon the

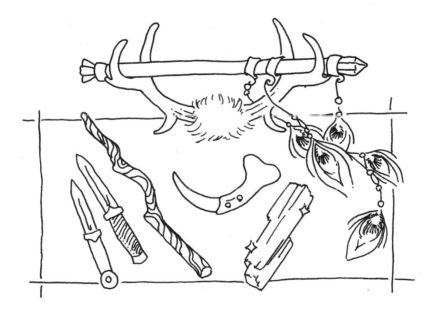

An assortment of athames and bollines might include items such as these black and white-handled knives, a sickle, and a crystal athame. Wands can be of oak, elder, or willow wood, or fennel stalks. A more elaborate wand could be made of a copper tube, filled with herbs and crystals, wrapped in leather or fur and decorated with feathers, amber, and jet. The one shown here is displayed on a set of deer antlers.

roots of the tree, of flower petals, or simply the arrangement of pebbles, shells, pine cones, or twigs as a pentacle at the roots of the tree. You could loosely tie a decorative ribbon to a branch, or simply state your appreciation and offer your blessing to the tree. The point is that you do not take the tree for granted. It is a living entity, and in this way the Green Craft is animistic—all things are seen as having an *anima*, or soul.

If you come across a stick that strikes you as energized, it could be a fairy gift to you, and you may use that for your wand. Leave something in the place where you found the stick.

Working/Herbal Knife

The bolline (bow-leen') is usually white handled and is the utility knife of the craft. This is the knife you use to cut your herbs, to inscribe your candles, and so forth. It should also be a three-sided blade like the athame. Nevertheless, this knife can be something as basic as a pocketknife. My first bolline when I was a child was a small pearl-handled pocket knife. My athame was a sword-shaped letter opener. Today there are sickle knives available in most occult shops and mail order catalogs. Some of these can be very attractive, and the sizes vary. There are some mail-order supply places listed in appendix 2. But, again, it is not necessary to expend a lot of money to practice witchcraft. The tools can be quite ordinary, except that you have energized them.

Another example of a bolline is a kitchen knife that is different from the one used as the athame. I have the paring knife for the athame, but the bolline from my kitchen tools is different. It is also wood handled, but is the one I use to level off the measurements in recipes. I find that with a variety of tools, when used consistently, each becomes saturated with specific energies that resonate when applied to particular tasks. For example, the kitchen tools are oriented to magical and ritual cooking (cookies, plum puddings, and fruitcakes for Yule, crescent cookies for Ostara, multi-grain buns for Lughnassadh, and so forth) while the altar tools are oriented to ritual and spell workings (creating the Circle, invocations, inscribing candles, and so forth).

Cauldron

The cauldron is another tool that typifies the witch. This object can vary substantially in size, material, and function. Most witches end up with quite a selection of cauldrons. The pot can be footed or not, made of iron, amalgamated metals, ceramic, or clay pottery. My favorite cauldron is a small pottery one that I use typically for candle magics with votive candles.

Incense, herbs, and twigs from trees can be burned in a cauldron, brews cooked, and candles burned, but I recommend that you designate which cauldrons you will use for food and which ones for magical stuffs. Some cauldrons are really pottery pots, sometimes supported on a metal tripod. Some metal ones have their own feet, while others have handles and are round on the bottom, being meant to hang from a fireplace sconce. You can even find fireplace settings with a pole, swing hook, and small iron pot hanging from it.

As with most of the other tools, there are expensive cauldrons and inexpensive ones. Check gift shops, occult supply shops, and catalogs. Or simply use a fireproof bowl or votive candle holder, such as you can find in a grocery store, for simple magics that will not create a fire hazard.

Extras

There are a number of other tools that can be used in the workings of the Craft. Altars can be created on a table top, a shelf, or bureau top. Or, you can use a stang, which is typical of Green Witchcraft. The stang may be a plain staff or a forked one. Wherever I have lived, a natural staff has come to me in the form of a long, plain, solid stick. This is one that I would use until I left an area, when I would return the staff to Nature. Now, however, I have a permanent stang with three prongs which I set into a star-shaped stand.

The staff or stang substitutes for the altar in a natural setting. You can decorate it with items from Nature when doing a ritual, then return the items to Nature. With a permanent stang, you may either leave the bark on or remove it, engrave it with runic symbols, drape it with herbal wreaths, wrap it with vines, hang from it feathers, beads, shells, or whatever expresses your personal style and taste.

Cups are used for ritual beverages, libations (offerings) to the Divine, and magic ceremonies. The cup may be metal, wood, pottery, or whatever you can find. A pretty wine glass may be used or a silver goblet, but a coconut shell also makes a fine cup, as does a

Cauldrons come in various shapes and materials—the only requirement is that they be able to contain your magical substances. Cups may be of glass, metal, pottery, and wood; bowls may contain salt, water, and libations; pentacles may be of wood, painted wood, and tile; various candles include tapers and votives; and a candle snuffer is useful.

deep sea shell. You can accumulate your tools with no expense by perusing what Nature has to offer, or you can seek them out in antique shops, rummage sales, thrift shops, grocery stores, craft shops, gift shops, occult stores, and catalogs.

Bowls are used for offerings, to hold water, and to hold salt or herbs in rituals. These can be pottery, brass, ceramic, or natural items such as seed pods or smaller shells. The amount of water and salt used in a ritual is rather small, so the items do not have to be very large.

Incense holders are also useful. There are brass one, ones that stand on a foot of some sort or hang from chains. There are those made for stick incense, long and with an opening in which to insert the end of the stick. These come in wood, glass, and ceramic, with some of the latter being quite ornate, in the shape of dragons or with figure pieces (where the stick is secured) representing scarabs, goddess images, and fairies. There are also those made for cone incense, such as the small brass pots of various shapes and sizes, typically from India. These usually have lids and perforations for air flow. A pot or large shell such as abalone are fine for bulk incense. A flat ceramic plate may also be used for cone or bulk incense.

Altar objects vary according to the intent of the practitioner. The altar should be expected to change in appearance depending on the season, the deity images invoked for a particular working, and the needs of the witch. There will be candles which may be set in candelabra, votive holders, candlesticks, or even sculpted crystals and rocks. There may be a pentacle of wood, ceramic, or brass, but you can create one on a piece of paper as well.

You may want to have figures of deities that appeal to your senses. A number of stores, even furniture stores, have deity images, and the catalogs listed in appendix 2 have fine images at reasonable prices. Even Nature can provide images. When we were camping near Jamestown on a Sabbat, I asked the Elementals (this is called "Speaking to the Wind") for images for our impromptu outdoor ritual, and in just a few moments of looking around the woods surrounding our campsite we found two pieces of wood that were perfect. I have kept these items and they evoke a very special memory and sensation for me of family gathering and participation. The natural image for the God is a horned deer-head shape; that of the Goddess appears as a mother holding a child. Other objects for the altar may be stones and other natural objects such as shells, feathers, and pieces of wood.

Some people like to use a bell to distinguish the various portions of the ritual. With the Green Craft, the bell may be used in this manner, reminiscent of the ancient images of the Goddess striking a bell. The bell is a Goddess accoutrement, although a bell is not necessary—clapping your hands is a fine substitute. Indeed, in working Fairy magics, the clapping of hands is better, or the tinkling of a tiny, tuneful brass bell.

Candles are used in the practice to quite an extent, and so a snuffer is probably a good tool to have. Some people prefer to pinch out their candles, but if the flame is particularly insistent, you could get burned. Also, if you are working candle magics in a small cauldron, for example, you will want a snuffer that can extinguish the candle flame that is probably going to be fed by herbs and such. A cookpot lid can be used for this if it blocks the air flow.

A pentacle is a good item to have as well. You may find these in catalogs or New Age/occult supply shops in wood, ceramic tile, and metal, or you can simply draw a star within a circle on a piece of paper within which to conduct your rituals. The pentacle is an object used to represent the Elemental Earth. The pentagram, the five-pointed star featured inside a circle on the pentacle, represents the Four Elementals and the Spirit, and hence, humankind. I have seen some very lovely pentacles with the star painted in a design entwined with vines, and others where the

markings are very straightforward and plain. Ceremonial pentacles may have a number of symbols inscribed about the star. Over
time, I have accumulated three pentacles I generally choose from
for my work, depending upon the intent.

**Several deity images are shown in this altar arrangement: three
candles: for the Lady and the Lord, with the center representing
both; statues; a sheaf of wheat and conch shell for the Lady (or
drift wood could be used); an oak branch and antlers for the Lord.
The elements are represented by a fossil for Earth, a crystal for
Air, lava for Fire, and amethyst for Water.**

Basic Altar/Working Area

Altar Arrangement

On the text pages 36 and 144, you will see a typical altar layout. The altar is laid out in three sections. As you face the altar, the left side is designated for the Goddess, the right side for the God, and the center portion is for both. In the Goddess section, you might place such items as a statue or goddess representation (be it a stone or a candle), water bowl, wine/juice goblet, wand, bell, and your herbal and oil supplies. The God section contains a representation of the deity (again, a candle or stone can be used instead of a statue), salt bowl, incense, athame, bolline, and such supplies as matches and candles. The center section is where you may place something to represent both deities, candle snuffer, censer, pentacle, cauldron, offering dish, libation bowl, book of rituals/spells (usually called the Book of Shadows), and spellworking materials. If you have bread or a small cake for the ritual, that can be placed on a plate at the right section of the altar.

Working Area (nondeity) Arrangement

There is also the method of using a nondeity working area arrangement. Not everyone has the space or opportunity to set up a little altar, and not everyone desires to conduct their practice of the Craft with the deities invoked, preferring the second style of practice, so there is an alternate arrangement for an altar. In this method of practice, you would set up your "working area" in the center of the table, desktop, or whatever you are using. Any area that is normally used for mundane activities should be wiped down, and a clean cloth (or placemat) placed on the surface. You can be as fancy or as plain as your needs or inclination allow.

Your tools should be symetrically laid out, and you can use a single candle, set toward the center back of the work space, for your focus. If you use two candles, set them to either side of the center of the work space, and you may also use a votive as a tool for spellwork. Your pentacle goes center and forward toward you a bit. The cauldron sits on top of the pentacle, knife to your right, wand to your left. Herbs, oils, cloth, string, feathers, stones, or other items you will be using can be placed to the left. Your Book of Shadows (or your written-out spell—notecards are handy) belongs at the center of your work area, below the pentacle. Incense is placed to the right of the pentacle.

Now that you have your tools and your altar arranged, you are ready to move to the next stage of magical practice—casting the circle. If room permits, you might want to set out four candles for the Elementals: Earth at the North, Air at the East, Fire at the South, and Water at the West of your circle. I begin each class by casting a circle, and use this as an opportunity to demonstrate different techniques and types of circles. In subsequent meetings, class members bring things for delineation of the circle and objects for the altar. We share a ritual of Cakes and Wine, usually with fruit juice, at the end of each class. The last class is rather like a "final exam" in which the students each take an active part in an Esbat or Sabbat ritual. They bring everything needed and prepare their own portion of the ritual. We spend time reviewing the previous lessons, having a question and answer session, and going into more detail in any segment of the previous classes that interested them before concluding the ritual and opening the circle. In a sense, for the weeks of class, we are a *learning coven*.

Class 2

Review of
Green Rules of Conduct;
Circle Casting; Assignment

Review

The Rules of Conduct

Try to remember the Rules of Conduct, then recite them quietly to yourself:

- Be careful what you do. (Think about what you are doing and what you want to attain before you begin a magical working.)

- Be careful who you trust. (Do you really know this person or is this someone who does not understand exactly what is going on with you and may use information against you?)

- Do not use The Power to hurt another because what is sent comes back. (Energies travel in circles.)

- Never use The Power against someone else who has The Power. (There is kinship between you and others who are connected with the Lady and the Lord of Witches.)

- To use The Power you must feel it in your heart and know it in your mind. (Accept what you know.)

Chapter One Quiz (answers on page 39)

1. Look for objects that you would use in delineating your personal circle. These can be crystals, rocks, items related to your favorite hobby or occupation, candles, and so on. Think about how you want your circle to appear—objects only at the Quarters; spread in a perimeter around you; a cord of colored silk or other natural material placed as a circle? Try a few different layouts to see what you find appealing. Your circle should be a place where you are "at home."

2. Answer the following questions:

   a. What does Green Witchcraft mean to you?

   _____

   _____

   _____

   b. What are the three styles of Green Witchcraft practice?
   1._____

   2._____

   3._____

   c. List the five Rules of Conduct.
   1._____

   2._____

   3._____

   4._____

   5._____

   d. What are two types of altars for a circle?
   1._____

   2._____

Circle Casting

Preparation

Prior to a formal casting of the ritual circle, you may lay out the items you will be using at the altar or work area. A relaxing bath with herbs such as lavender, rosemary, thyme, and vervain, tied in a muslin or a layered cheesecloth pouch (like a cloth teabag), will soothe you while awakening your senses at the same time. Then robe as you prefer for your work. Some people like to work sky-clad (in the nude), others like to wear a robe similar to those of monks, and others have special clothes they like to wear for ritual.

Light the candles at the altar, then wave the match or blow on it to extinguish the match flame. Next, light the incense at the altar. If you are using stick incense, light the tip with a match and shake or blow out the match. Watch the flame at the tip of the incense wand, and when you see a red area on it (this takes only a moment or two), shake the wand to extinguish the flame, or blow it out. The red area will continue to smolder and release the smokey incense into the air. If you are using an incense cone, you do pretty much the same thing. It might give you better control to hold the cone by the broader base as you light the tip, but you can also get it started (usually) by lowering the lighted match to the cone tip and holding it there until the cone ignites. When you see the redness, the incense is lit and you can extinguish the flame.

When using a charcoal block and incense that is in resin or powder form, or dry herbs, a pair of small (sugar cube) tongs makes a handy little tool, allowing you to hold the charcoal block in the tongs with one hand while you light the charcoal with a match in the other or by holding an edge of the charcoal in a candle flame. Otherwise, set the block in the burner and try to light it at one side. The block will spark and sputter at first, and you may need to fan it a little (the feather is another handy tool for working with incense) to make the block catch. Once it is glowing, you can drop bits of incense or herbs on top to smolder. Too much at once, and you may suffocate the block, so go easy on the resins, powders, and herbs until you get a feel for how well the block is working.

Not all blocks work well, and sometimes you might come across a defective one. If you are determined to use loose herbs, and cannot get anywhere with a charcoal block, you can light a bundle of herbs in a dish or shell, or use the herbs in a votive candle as part of your spell working. This will burn very hot, so be sure your candle container is fireproof, set on a fireproof/scorch-proof surface, and you have something handy to set over the container to smother the flame when you are done. Lining the container with sand helps prevent heat damage. Watch out for long dangling locks of hair, drooping sleeves, shawls, and so forth when working with incense, candles, and burning herbs.

Cauldrons and incense holders—incense comes in sticks, bundles, cones, resins, and dried herbs.

28

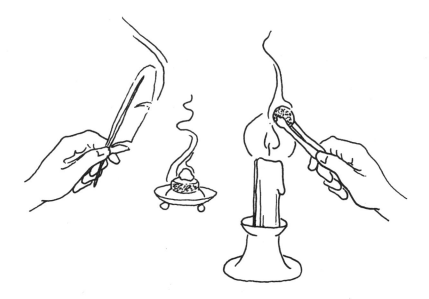

Incense burning with charcoal. Use a feather to fan the flame until the block is lighted, then waft the smoke about with the feather.

Another way to light any incense is with the flame of the central candle on the altar/work area. You simply hold the incense to the candle flame, let it ignite, wave or blow it out, and set the incense in its proper holder. By far, the stick and cone incense is the easiest to use, but I do love the aroma of frankincense and dragonsblood resins. Remember that charcoal consumes oxygen and releases fumes, so be sure to use an airy location.

Creating the Circle

This comes after you have arranged your altar, and there are some very basic steps to creating the circle, which is your sacred space. The purpose of the circle is to contain the raised energy so you can then focus it and direct it to accomplishing your particular goal. You create the circle prior to spellwork, Sabbat rituals, and Esbat celebrations. In ceremonial circles as described in the grimoires, the idea is more to keep demons at bay. Green Witchcraft does not subscribe to demons, Satan, or any other negative images from modern religions, so the function of the circle is to give you a cleansed area where you create a sacred site, what some call a temple. Here you call upon The Power, raise energy for a goal, focus it, direct it, and send it to work for you.

Not all circles need to be formally created as shown if you need only a momentary calm space. You could visualize your circle, for example, draw it in the dirt, make it by pointing your finger, and so forth, depending upon where you are at the time. Some circles are created for protection against ill influences around you, others for raising and projecting energy to accomplish a goal, others simply for the peace of meditation.

The first thing you will normally do in a ritual or formal spell-working is sweep the area of the circle. This delineates the space of the circle. Check tab "Basic Ceremony" on pages 145–148 of the text and read through the steps. When sweeping the circle, you may want to say as you move around the circle:

> *I sweep clean the circle, sweeping negativity and chaotic energies away from my sacred space.*

Next you light candles and incense, then announce your intent to actually create the circle. With this announcement, you are stating that this is something you do of your own free will—no one is forcing you—and alert your subconscious mind as well as The Power.

You may want to take a light to the points of the Quarters (north, east, south, and west of your circle) to express these areas as prepared for your later calling of the Elementals, but it is not necessary. In each case, you would be calling for light in relation to an attribute of the Elemental represented at that particular place on the circle, seeking to merge an Elemental attribute (strength, inspiration or enlivening, warmth, and cleansing) with light. You may vary the wording shown on text page 146 or change it according to the type of moon in an Esbat celebration, for example. Different aspects of the Elementals, and different aspects of light are utilized for Fairy rituals, Dark Moon rituals, and Dark Power spellworkings (*Green Witchcraft II: Balancing Light and Shadow* has more information on these rituals and magical workings). These variations will be covered when we talk more in depth about the Elementals.

Next, you actually designate the circle, with the altar area inside the circle. See step 5 in the text—you may use the athame, beginning at the north, moving east, then south, then west, and returning to the north, or you may use your "power hand" (the one you favor), or you may use a staff, sword, or wand. The tool that fits for you is the one to use—the fluctuations of energy are sometimes very subtle, but you may sense that there is a particular tool you *need* to use that you might not normally use. Trust your instincts and, later on, you may discover there was a reason for your feeling. Generally, though, you use the knife to create the circle and the wand to call upon the Elementals and the Divine.

In this section of the text is the sample wording in which the Goddess and the God are mentioned when the tool is "sanctioned" for circle-making when raised up at the altar, then lowered as you walk (or motion around the circle, if there is not sufficient room to move around). For nondeity ritual, you may want to change "I draw this circle in the presence of the Goddess and the God . . ." to:

> *I draw this circle to be a sacred space where The Power may manifest and bless me.*

As you walk around the circle, envision a flow of energy passing from the earth through your feet and up your body. The energy moves as a blue light down your arm, out of your power hand and through the tool you are holding to form a line of energy marking the perimeter of the circle as you walk it. When working indoors, I like to say:

This is the boundary of the circle, around me, through walls and floors and furniture, above me and below me as a sphere is the circle cast and consecrated to the Lady and the Lord that they may manifest and bless their child.

Envision the circle as a sphere surrounding you with contained energy, unpenetrable by outside or disruptive energies, where you can concentrate on your Craft working.

By deleting references to the Goddess and the God, you are essentially invoking The Power from within, calling up energy from the earth to work through you in your focus. The Power may be defined as Lady and Lord, or not, depending on your style of practice.

Now that the circle area has been swept and light invoked, you need to cleanse the sacred space. The example in the text uses the Divine presence, but you can stop prior to that:

Salt is necessary to life and is purifying. I bless this salt to be used in this sacred space.

For a nondeity oriented procedure, use the athame to drop three bits of salt into the water bowl, and stir three times, while saying:

Let the blessed salt purify this water that it may be consecrated to cleanse this sacred circle.

Take the bowl and walk deosil (clockwise) around the circle (N–E–S–W, and back to N), sprinkling the circle:

I consecrate this circle with the power of the blessed salt and hallowed water. The circle is conjured a circle of power that is purified and sealed. So Mote It Be!

That last phrase means, "So must it be" which seals the energy of the intent. It is often used in the Craft at the end of a spell to seal the spell. In essence, you are recognizing a change, and by doing so, have made the change real and complete.

Return the bowl to the altar, take up the incense holder, and waft the smoke around the circle. Here is when you might want to use a large feather to help move the incense around the circle as you pace the boundary. You could say:

With this fragrant smoke do I honor the Elementals and enhance the power of this circle.

The circle is ready; now you need only to consecrate yourself for working within the circle (text page 147). You may use anointing oil, or spring water, or the blessed water you created for the circle. With your fingertip, draw on your forehead a symbol that you feel is suitably reverent—a solar cross, lunar spiral (these two can be combined), a pentagram, infinity sign (numeral 8, on its side), horned moon, crescent moon, sun circle with a dot in the center, life circle (representing the cycle of birth, death, and rebirth), and so forth.

The text example can be altered to:

I am consecrated by The Power within this circle.

When you cleansed the circle and censed it, you already brought the essence of the Elementals into your work. Salt represents Earth, water is for Water, the fire of the incense is for Fire, the scented smoke for Air, so you are now ready to formally call upon the presence of the Elementals to aid in your work. The invocation, with wand in hand, on text page 147 is simple, yet effective. Many Traditions draw the design of the pentagram in the air, beginning at a different point for calling upon each Elemental and farewelling each Elemental (typically called Summoning and Banishing—but I feel those words are inappropriate for the Elementals, who are kin, after all). This is really a ceremonial inclusion to witchcraft and not necessary. Once you become familiar with working with the Elementals, the conversation is open whenever you want, and no circle is needed for communication. It is very similar to prayer, but without a set format.

Your invocation in the Green Craft is respectful and familial. You remind yourself of the connection between yourself and the Elementals, and you would address them as you would address yourself. Earth is in your body and physical strength; Air is in you breath and thought; Fire is in the energy of your cells, feeding on life to create life, and in the power of your drive and determination; Water is in your blood, body fluids, and represents your flowing emotions.

After walking to each cardinal point (north, east, south, and west) of the circle, and calling upon the Elemental of that realm to attend your rite, you may return to the altar, set down the wand and pick up the knife to draw the symbol of working between the worlds—the symbol of infinity (8 on its side), or the runic symbol of breakthrough (a squared off 8 on its side). If not working with deity imagery, simply change the wording to something like:

> ### Hail to the Elementals at the four quarters! I stand between the worlds with love and power all around!

You need not make a libation to the Divine as part of the circle ceremony, but you may do so to honor The Power and the Elementals. Follow text example. Simply pour a bit of beverage from your cup into the libation bowl or cauldron, and then take a sip for yourself. You are ready to do whatever you need to in the circle, be it a spell, ritual, etc. I like to create a "learning circle" in my class, and you may want to do so as you work through this course. Cast the circle, then ask the Elementals for aid in your learning when you call them at the Quarters. Work for awhile, then when you are ready to stop, farewell the Elementals as will be shown, and open the circle.

When working in your own residence, you may want to create a permanent circle. This may be accomplished by having a room set aside for your magical practice. In a place where the atmosphere and environment is purely intended as your sacred space, the area will take on a special feel, which you can renew and reenergize from time to time by asperging (sprinkling) the area with a sprig of purple heather dipped in spring water (bottled is fine if that is all that is available to you) and burning an incense such as frankincense or sage and sweetgrass.

While within the circle you perform lessons, meditations, spellwork, divinations, and Sabbat or Esbat celebrations. When a Sabbat falls on an Esbat, I like to do the Esbat and any spellwork needed, then move into the Sabbat ritual, so the two rituals can be combined if desired. You may create the circle for simple devotionals such as lighting incense and candles at the altar, and have a quiet time in which to offer your reverence to the Divine, or to release tensions and nervous energy into the ground and find the calmness within. In witchcraft, this is called grounding and centering yourself, and it is what you do before a Craft activity so that the energy flow is smooth.

After spell work, meditation, divinations, and such, you will want to again ground and center yourself so that the excess energy is released, otherwise you may be agitated and become easily upset. You may do this by envisioning the excess energy as sparkles that dance close around you, and you let the sparkles gather and roll down your arms, then touch the ground with your palms and see the energy flow back into the earth. Once you feel the energy of your body is back in balance, you can remove your hands from the ground and stand again.

Parting

Once the circle is no longer needed (you have concluded your ritual or purpose for drawing the circle) you should prepare for parting company with the Elementals and other energies and entities you have called upon or that have been attracted to the activities, so you will be ready to open the circle. To begin your parting, you need to be ready to move back into ordinary awareness. One way to accomplish this is through the Cakes and Wine ceremony, with a snack and beverage of your choice. Refer to text page 156 for a sample of this ritual. Eating a snack and taking a drink of something helps your conscious mind to return to the forefront and alerts your body that you are returning to a normal state of being. The ritual of joining knife into cup relates to the communion rituals of mainstream churches—the beverage represents the waters of life, the knife the energy of life, or more directly, the Goddess and the God. For nondeity practice, hold up the cup and plate of food, saying:

> *Food and beverage, staples of life and waters of life, united through the fire of the sun and the breath of the air, I accept these gifts of Nature and remember that I am part of the cycle of life.*

This is a good time to chat and socialize with anyone who may be working with you, as in a class setting, or to gather your thoughts and perhaps even jot down a note or two about your activity in the circle. When you have refreshed yourself, it is the time of parting. Holding your knife horizontally over the altar, you can use text page 157 or something like:

> *I am blessed by the powers* (or say "Elementals") *that watch and protect me, guiding me here and in all things. I came in love and I depart in love.*

Now raise the knife as in a salute to honor the rites of the Craft. You are recalling the links between yourself and the practice of the Craft, reminding yourself of the common thread that unites you with other witches:

> *Love is the law and love is the bond. Merry did I* (or "we" if working with others) *meet, merry do I part, and merry will I meet again. Merry meet, merry part, merry meet again! The circle is cleared. So Mote It Be!*

Before opening the circle, you need to walk around it again and farewell the Elementals. If you have set out candles at the Quarters, you will be snuffing them out after you address the

Elemental of that Quarter. With farewelling, you can also reiterate the kind of help you want from each Elemental if you have worked on a spell, or you may want to express your joy of unity with the individual Elementals. The basic text on page 157 is simple and direct. If no candles were lit, and you are not encumbered with a candle snuffer, you may want to hold your wand in your power hand as you farewell them, with open arms raised up:

> *Depart in peace, Elemental Earth! My blessings take with you!*

Lower and close your arms, move to the next Quarter and continue until you are again facing the altar at the north. Now you will set down your tools on the altar, raise up your hands and farewell any Others who may have been drawn to your circle to lend you their energy or simply to watch:

> *Beings and powers of the visible and invisible, depart in peace! You aid in my work, whisper in my mind, and bless me from Otherworld, and there is harmony between us. My blessings take with you. The circle is cleared. So Mote It Be!*

This is the second time you have stated that the circle is cleared, but like most things in magic, this is said in threes, three being considered a number of conclusion or binding.

Opening the Circle

The circle is opened with the same tool used to draw it, usually this will be the athame. Since, to draw it, you walked clockwise from north to east to south to west, to open it, you do the reverse. Beginning at the north, you walk or motion to the west, then south, then east, and back to the north, envisioning the energy that you sent out as a blue light now returning to you through your tool or power hand. As you walk or indicate the circle opening, you may say the following:

The circle is open, yet the circle remains as its magical power is drawn back into me.

When you return to your starting point, see the light dancing around the blade of the knife, and return the light and power to within yourself by touching the flat of the blade against your forehead, sealing your circle within.

Now you state the clearing of the circle for the third time to bind it as so, as on text page 158—or for nondeity workings, say:

The ceremony is ended, the circle is cleared and withdrawn. Blessings have been given and blessings have been received. May the peace of unity with Nature and with the Power remain in me. So Mote It Be.

This is your statement of ending. Everything is concluded, and you return to the normal world. Touch the ground with your palms if you feel overly energized. Clean up the basic altar or work area, put away your tools, dispose of libations by pouring out onto the ground, on a potted plant, or even rinsing the liquid down the sink, while envisioning the libation as moving with the water to the sea. Spellworking materials may now be tidied up and put away while crafted items placed as intended (a protection charm in your car, for example).

Assignment

1. Review the first two chapters of the textbook.

Answers to Questions

2a. The Green Craft is herbal; it means working through nature; is the basic, foundational level of witchcraft; involves working directly with the powers of the Elementals and the Divine; is Natural Witchcraft; is the religious level of the Norse system ruled by the Lady and the Lord (Goddess and God) of Nature rather than by deities of social classes; and is an expression of the Old Religion.

2b. 1. Within a mainstream religious system using folk magics, deity/saint names.

2. Without any religious/deity reference using the natural powers of the Elementals and your own/Nature's energies.

3. As a religion honoring a dual deity of Goddess and God with a self-initiation and later with a self-dedication.

2c. 1. Be careful what you do

2. Be careful who you trust

3. Do not use The Power to hurt another because what is sent comes back

4. Never use The Power against someone else who has The Power

5. To use The Power you must feel it in your heart and know it in your mind

2d. 1. Basic Altar.

2. Working Area.

Class 3

Review, Casting a Learning Circle; Meditation & Technique

Review

Rules of Conduct

I always begin my classes with a review of the Rules of Conduct. Since you are using a course handbook, without going back into the last lesson or the textbook, see if you can recite the five Rules of Conduct. Turn back to the end of the previous class and compare the Rules you recited to the answers listed under 2c (p. 39). Did you miss any? If so, softly repeat the rules two or three times aloud so you can hear the words as well as see them.

Learning Techniques

People learn in various ways—through reading, writing, recitation, and hearing—and each person has an affinity to one of these techniques. Since the Rules of Conduct will form the core for your practice of Green Witchcraft, this is an opportunity for you to try the different techniques for memorization. Think of the meanings for the rules, referring to the first class if you need help. As you recite the Rules of Conduct, you should be developing a feel for how they apply to you and the style of practice with which you are comfortable.

Casting the Learning Circle

Setting Up an Altar/Working Area

The best way to study the Craft is in a setting that enhances your senses to the magic and power of witchcraft. In my classes, besides casting a variety of types of circles, I also set up a different style of altar each time we meet in order to demonstrate a number of options for magical practice. You may want to try this yourself. Create an altar or working area in what will be the northern end or center of your circle (yes, that's next). You may refer to text page 36 for an example if you like. This will be your altar/working area and should reflect your own taste and style. Remember that simple objects in nature make excellent tools and altar objects. You should have salt (or burdock/dandelion root) and spring or fresh water in bowls, also incense, and at least one candle.

Sometimes people ask me how they can tell which way is north, and usually they groan and make a face when they realize how simple it is. To find North, find the sun. The sun rises in the East and sets in the West. Before noon, the sun is in the Eastern part of the sky, after noon, the Western part of the sky. If in the East, face the sun, and North is off your left shoulder. If the sun is in the West, face the sun, and North is off your right shoulder. Or, use a simple compass. Most people are familiar with where the sun rises and sets in relation to their homes, however, so the guide is simple and effective.

Variation of Circle-casting

The next thing to construct is the "learning circle." There are a number of ways to cast a circle. In the first class we looked at the tabbed section, "Basic Ceremony," in the text and made changes for nondeity circle casting. In both cases, there was a lot of equipment used—incense, water, candles, knife, wand, cup, beverage, food, and so forth. Let us try a different style now. You have laid out your altar/working area, so you are ready to begin. I will be referring to the altar from here on out, but if you are using a working area, substitute the word as you read.

Sweep the circle area with a besom clockwise—deosil—which means that your movements will begin at the North, proceed to the East, then South, then West. You can say as you sweep:

> *As I sweep, may the besom chase away all negativity from within this circle, that it may be cleared and ready for my work.*

Light the incense and your altar candle(s), then clap your hands three times and state:

> *The circle is about to be cast and I freely stand within to work and learn in this class.*

Take the center candle of the altar (you may only have one candle on the altar, and this is fine to use) and hold up the candle at the Quarters of North, East, South, and West, saying:

> *I call upon Light and Earth at the North to illuminate and strengthen the circle.*
> *I call upon Light and Air at the East to illuminate and enliven the circle.*
> *I call upon Light and Fire at the South to illuminate and warm the circle.*
> *I call upon Light and Water at the West to illuminate and cleanse the circle.*

Back at the North, raise your knife (athame, power hand, or wand) and state:

> *I draw this circle in the presence of the powers of the earth, sky, sun, and sea (or the Lady and the Lord) that they may aid and bless me in my studies.*

Walk around the circle deosil, with the knife lowered to delineate the perimeter of the circle. Envision a blue light shooting out from the point and forming the boundary as you say:

> *This is the boundary of the circle, around me, through walls and floors, above me and below me as a sphere is the circle cast and consecrated to the powers of Nature and the universe that they may work with me. This learning circle is charged that only love shall enter and leave.*

Circle Ritual Preferences

At this point you have created the circle. You could stop here and begin with the rest of the lesson, or continue as described in the last class. Your candles are already lit, the incense is burning, and you have called upon the light at the quarters. Return to the altar, set down your knife, and clap your hands three times. You are ready to study.

If doing the rest of the ritual as covered in the last class, refer to the lesson or the text tabbed "Basic Ceremony." Now is when you would touch the athame to the salt (burdock or dandelion root) to bless it, then add the salt to the water in blessing. You would then sprinkle the circle with the water to purify and seal the circle, and then take the incense around the circle to cense it. If you want to use anointing oil to consecrate yourself inside the circle, you would do that next. You would then take your wand and address the Elementals at the Quarters. Page 147 of the text gives suggestions for envisioning the Elementals, but use what comes to mind for you. For example, you might prefer to envision a lion or a phoenix for the South, a bear or wolf for the North, and so forth. Next, you would draw above the altar the symbol for working between the worlds, do the welcoming and the libation, clap three times (or ring a bell), and then you will be ready to proceed with the lesson.

Meditation and Techniques

Purpose

Meditation is one of the first aspects of the Craft you will want to work on to learn about focusing energy. Much of meditation is directed at finding an inner calm, your center, as it were. Through meditation we are able to connect with the various aspects of the earth as part of a cohesive entity—animal, mineral, plant, water, clouds, sky, and so on, and acquire the sense of being part of Gaia, the living organism of Earth. From here, meditation can take you beyond Gaia and it becomes a primary step to union with the universe, the cosmos. Through meditation, you can learn to traverse the boundaries of the three dimensions, of time, and of space. Pretty impressive, yes? Well, meditative journeys can be impressive, but they tend to be singular. This means that your travels will most likely be solitary unless you have a really compatible partner or a guide.

There are different kinds of meditative journeys. A shamanic journey is undertaken to travel to near death in an effort to save another person, help that person find his or her way into the Shadowland, or to gain esoteric knowledge. This is the vision-questing style of meditation that requires fasting and isolation. People who embark on these journeys do so with varying degrees of success. I have heard of some marvelous experiences from vision-questing. However I do not recommend it for the average student unless working *with* another experienced person. In a shamanic journey, at least two people should work together so that one may watch out for the safety of the other.

You can also visit other planes and worlds where you may encounter different peoples and different ways of thinking. What exactly does visiting other planes and worlds mean? These are travels to Otherworld, the realm of Faerie or the Other People; to Underworld or Shadowland, the realm of the dead or the unborn;

to Summerland, a place of transition from Underworld rest to Otherworld or rebirth in Middleworld, the realm we normally consider our physical home. Yet even the term "physical" is difficult to interpret. Spiritual entities can move objects, can manifest, and can seem very solid and "real" (as in angelic appearances, ghostly visits, the appearance of helpers in dire situations, and so on), so it requires an expansion of awareness to recognize that the hard-edged terms we normally think in are really not so easy to pin down.

There are those who consider any meditative travel as purely a figment of the traveler's imagination. Yet, it is from our imaginations that reality is manifested. All inventions began as imaginings, for example. All ideas come from the realm of imagination before they are translated into the realm of physical existence. This transition is described in the tarot cards as the movement of ideas from the realm of the moon into that of the sun, so if you have both these cards in a setting, particularly one with knights/princes (thoughts) in it, you are looking at manifesting your ideas. By entering into an altered state of awareness you will be able to move between the worlds with ease whenever you wish and access the power and knowledge of these other worlds in your daily life.

You can access the inner visions of the mind to solve problems and find answers to your questions. Meditation can enhance your ability to learn by helping you achieve alternative states of being, opening your awareness, and training your mind to focus. But meditation also promotes good health by giving you a time to calm your mind and soothe your nervous system. This process switches off the mundane or routine consciousness in order to let the subconscious or intuitive self take over. The subconscious is opened up to stimulate the conscious with new approaches to life situations.

Green Witchcraft Types of Meditation

There are different intentions for the use of meditation, such as that of Shamanic intercession for healing, for seeking a spiritual guide, or for expressing your oneness with the universal power. You may want to link yourself to the powers of the earth in a sense of union, identity, and communication. Meditation can be used to put yourself in another person's shoes for empathetic understanding. This section of the Manual may be studied further in conjunction with chapter 5 of *Green Witchcraft II: Balancing Light and Shadow.*

By uniting with objects in Nature or with creatures for oneness you are gaining an awareness based on the perspective of the animal or object. You begin by envisioning typical characteristics of the object or animal. You may even want to practice becoming the object or animal to better sense what that perspective is like. Soon, you will be able to merge with the subject, seeing with the subject's eyes and sensing with the subject's sensations—even a boulder "feels" the warmth of the sun, the damp pounding of the rain, and the intrusive network of hair-like roots holding moss and lichen in place.

This sort of motion should be done with care. Do not do this with people unless they give their consent, and be cautious with animals so as not to startle them. Kindly intent is necessary, for that is what an animal senses first. From the new perspective, you can pay attention to the different view, and even see yourself looking at the subject. With gentle blending, you can pick up on what an animal is feeling, and you can even project images to the animal and return to yourself to see the reaction.

By linking yourself through meditation with other life-forms, you are able to communicate with them. This makes the language barrier vanish, and dispels the sensation of fear. By being "one" with the creatures of Nature, you may pass as one, with a sense of community and peace. With a household pet (particularly cats) you accept that they can speak to you directly. My experience with cats is that they are highly telepathic with one another, and if they are accustomed to you and know that you respect them as individuals, they will communicate with you. Often what you receive are images rather than "words."

Why do I feel cats are telepathic? As one example, I saw one of my seven cats in a precarious position, struggling to get a better grip. Without her making a sound, the rest of the cats from the household came from all directions to watch in silent concentration. The first cat seemed to visibly calm, and carefully picked her way from her perch to a firm footing, then the other cats (who are her mother and litter mates) all dispersed again to whence they had come. I felt they gave her supportive energy and directions after she called to them for help.

Cats, often found as familiars, are highly telepathic.

My daughter and I have both had experiences where we ask a cat a question, either out loud or simply in a questioning thought, and we have received very distinct images in reply. On one occasion, my daughter saw the cats looking intently through the screen of the back porch, but she could see nothing exceptional in the yard to hold their attention. She asked them what they were looking at, and the image of a black snake coiled in a flower pot came to her. She went outside the porch and found that there was indeed a black snake in an empty flower pot near the back porch.

I have heard a cat pawing at the back door to come in and simply wondered who could still be outside, since I was certain they were all indoors, and immediately saw in my mind the exact cat that was at the door. There are other people who have told me of their "telepathic" encounters with their cats, and I feel that this ability of cats and humans to connect is what made these graceful creatures so special to the ancient Egyptians and later to witches in general.

Meditation is also used to travel, be it in the simple matter of stargazing at night, to carefully prepared cosmic motion with the visualization of moving through the atmosphere and into space until the sense of up and down becomes meaningless. Beyond this there is the meditative motion of astral travel. This is also called "leaving your body." It is rather like a sudden leap of consciousness, where you move like a shot into the highest confining corner of a room and look back to see yourself below. For some people, the shock of this kind of travel is sufficient to return them instantly to their bodies. The sensation is rather like jumping into a swimming pool rather than easing yourself in. You can either stay and acclimate, or jump back out. But, if you practice the technique of letting go gently, you will be able to leave with less shock and then begin to travel. This too, takes getting used to, since knowing where you want to go will cause you to rapidly arrive. Not all of astral travel is to other planes. Out-of-body experiences often take a person to places in the present and, in some cases, a person will be seen by those who are sensitive. People may interact with an astral traveler only to be shocked when the traveler vanishes, returning to their physical body.

Creative meditations combine communication and astral connection. This includes such things as meditative writing, when you simply let go with pen and paper and your writing flows. Singing, composition, and painting may also come with the altered state of awareness of meditation. So may speaking in tongues, divination, and healing.

It is always most productive to prepare for a creative meditation, planning the desired communication in advance. You may want to call upon the Elementals or The Power to give you direction in a specific area, be it problem-solving or poetry, writing, musical composition, or creative projects. At the end of your session, you should note what happened in a journal for later review. Always ground and center yourself once you are finished with a meditation, to bring yourself back into balance in the physical plane.

I also enjoy creative meditation experiences as a spontaneous offering or gift to the Divine. I have gazed at the Full Moon, thinking of the Lady, then begun singing an unknown melodious song using words whose meanings were felt, in honor of the Goddess. It becomes my gift to her, and yet she has filled me with her presence. This is the joy of unity. In seeking an inner awareness of some matter, I have called upon the Lord when I had paper and pen, and found my answer came easily in a brief essay or a poetic form of rhyming quatrains with a meter of fourteen beats per line. The poems are usually very personal and I rarely share them, being satisfied to simply keep them in a journal. Sometimes I use such a poem or essay as a reading at a Sabbat ritual.

Meditative Process

Meditation works by switching off the routine consciousness to let your intuitive or subconscious self take over for a time in a safe, or protected, atmosphere. This allows for an alternate state of awareness to come into being. There are different techniques, and you may develop your own, but the easiest to start with is to sit comfortably in a quiet place where you will not be disturbed for twenty to thirty minutes. You may sit in a chair with your feet flat on the floor with legs uncrossed as this would quickly become uncomfortable and distracting. Place your hands at rest in your lap or on your knees.

Some people prefer to sit on the floor or a cushion, keeping the spine straight for the smooth flow of energy. Having a particular rug or cushion that you always sit on during meditations will act as a trigger to your mind after awhile, so that simply unrolling the rug or bringing out the pillow becomes part of your personal ritual and sets your mind started toward the meditative state. On the floor, you could sit in a yogic or semi-yogic position with one leg slightly unbent. Whatever way you sit, the main concern is that you are comfortable and that you do not have to move around because of soreness, cramping, or limbs falling asleep from constricted circulation of the blood. These are the kinds of things that will interfere with your meditation if you are not properly prepared.

You may want to light a candle and/or incense, play some soothing and unobtrusive music on a tape or CD, and create your circle for a peaceful and undisturbed setting. Close your eyes and relax. Let the tensions of the day drain away, feeling them collecting from around your body, then flowing to your arms and legs to drip from your hands and feet into the floor, dissipating into the nurturing earth.

Let your extraneous thoughts filter away. This is one of the harder things to master when first starting in meditation. You will hear all kinds of "mind chatter" and find your mind drifting to the little chores you need to do around the house—the laundry, the dishes, and so forth. You will have to get past this. Focus on a candle, or on your tummy as you watch yourself breathing. Breathing is how you can move into the meditative state.

Breathe deeply, inhaling to the count of two, then hold that breath for one count, and exhale for two counts. By steady breathing and focusing on this basic effort, you will silence the conscious mind. When you are in a restful state, you can then address the purpose of the meditation. If you are working on problem solving or creativity, focus on a word or a question that needs an answer. You may want to use a guided meditation. You can buy pre-recorded meditation tapes to play when you are relaxed, or you can read and tape your own, then play it back when you are feeling serene.

With a guided meditation, let your mind see the images described. You have to be willing to go where the voice is taking you. Visualizations help you to enter an altered state where you can comprehend that time, space, and what is considered reality exist only as you perceive them to be. Therefore, they are not boundaries, but are unlimited or even nonexistent—as you choose. When the session is over, ground yourself by touching the floor and letting the residual energy drain away. Take something to eat or drink, then move into doing a routine chore to get yourself focused. You may want to keep a journal of your meditations to keep track of your development.

Ritual Meditation

Ritual meditation differs from other meditations through the use of the circle, and calling of the Elementals. When I suggested that you might want to use incense and a candle, these are part of a ritual meditation format; but more importantly, the meditation is meant to have a magical purpose or intent. This means that the color of the candle should be appropriate to the purpose of the meditation. Refer to the text tab "Colors" (page 63–64). Here is a listing of colors and the various associations for those colors. Text pages 57–59 list herbs for incenses that may used for various goals. Select an incense or burn herbs that match your purpose.

Drumming lightly or shaking a rattle may be an aid to free the mind for meditation as well. This draws the mind's focus with restful, repetitive sounds. Once the meditation or visualization is begun, the drumming or rattle shaking may cease, and this is fine. When the meditation is over, again you will ground and center, then extinguish the candle, farewell the Elementals, open the circle, and return to some daily routine.

In the last assignment, you were asked to find things you would use in delineating your personal circle. For a ritual meditation, you could lay these out in a circle around your meditation space. You may mark off your circle with stones, nuts, crystals, or other objects that relate to the essence of your objective in the ritual. The Elementals can be represented at the quarters by different objects (a shell, a nut, a stone, a feather, a piece of lava or fired clay) or colored candles. Light a central candle near you for your focus, but not so close as to be distracting. Call upon the Elementals to aid you in your meditation, stating what it is you seek to accomplish, then drop a few herbs into the candle flame—mugwort is excellent, as is any herb from the listing that matches your purpose.

With ritual meditation, you are envisioning the reality you desire, and discovering the manner of bringing it into being. The circle provides a sacred space with a sense of comfort and repose. In rituals and spells, the circle is created to contain the raised energy so it can be focused and directed, but in a ritual meditation, the circle provides a haven from which to explore outward on inner and Otherworldly planes. The following format calls upon the Elementals to aid in the meditation. The four Elementals are the four essences of life: Earth, Air, Fire, and Water, with the first two as aspects of the God, and the last two as aspects of the Goddess.

To cast a general meditation circle, light an incense such as frankincense or sandalwood, and light a purple candle in a candlestick or other holder that you will be able to carry around the circle. Purple is symbolic of spiritual renewal, but you could select a different color according to your needs.

If outdoors, with a wand, stick, twig, athame, or the index finger of your power hand, walk in a circle around your meditation area, drawing a ring around yourself in the ground. If indoors, do the same, but envision the ring being drawn on the floor. As the circle is drawn, envision the energy of the Earth coming up through your body and shooting out as a blue light from the tool or finger you are using to delineate the circumference of the magic sphere around you.

Walk counterclockwise (widdershins) to signify that you are moving into another realm as you form your meditation ring. Start at the North to emphasize the realm of wisdom and Otherworldly travels. As you create the circle, say:

> *The circle is drawn as a circle of power around me,*
> *above me, and below me in a sphere that passes*
> *through all boundaries in all planes* (cast and consecrated to the Lady and the Lord and) *charged by the*
> *Elemental powers!*

Set down the tool used to draw the circle and take up the incense; walk around the ring and waft the incense smoke as you say:

> *This circle is cleansed and purified by the pleasing*
> *aroma of incense.*

Set the incense near your focus candle at the north of the circle. Take up the candle now and go to the North. The candle is your beacon to the Elementals. Hold up the candle and say:

I welcome thee, Elemental Earth, to my circle. As I have flesh and bone, we are kith and kin, and I call upon you to watch over me, aid, and guide me in my travels.

Move to the West, hold up the candle, and say:

I welcome thee, Elemental Water, to my circle. As I have water and blood, we are kith and kin, and I call upon you to watch over me, aid, and guide me in my travels.

Move to the South, hold up the candle and say:

I welcome thee, Elemental Fire, to my circle. As I have passion and energy, we are kith and kin, and I call upon you to watch over me, aid, and guide me in my travels.

Move to the East, hold up the candle and say:

I welcome thee, Elemental Air, to my circle. As I have thought and breath, we are kith and kin, and I call upon you to watch over me, aid, and guide me in my travels.

Set the candle down next to the incense, and sit comfortably in the center of the circle, facing North. Breathe deeply and exhale, repeat. Now begin the simple breathing exercise of inhaling for two counts, holding for one, and releasing for two counts, etc. When the conscious mind becomes still, you are ready to open the subconscious mind and access the universe, so it is not unusual for the perceived surroundings to change. Don't be disturbed by this, simply move with the experience. The Elementals will look after you.

At this point you may either bring to mind a word or question, or move into a guided meditation. You could also visualize or focus on a card with a word sigil. A sigil is made by taking a key word that you have chosen for your meditation focus and drawing lines on a witch's sigil wheel. The wheel (see illustration, p. 57) can be copied onto a piece of paper. One continuous line is drawn to each letter. The initial letter is designated by a circle, the ending letter by a curb. In the case of double letters or letters used twice in a word, the line must remain distinct for each letter. While the line you draw may cross itself several times, depending on the word, each letter is indicated individually. The line may intersect, but does not go back over itself (see examples).

In a ritual meditation, you begin by envisioning what is for you a comfortable, secure place. I have heard of temple scenes, forests, meadows, cabins in the woods, and caves as typical starting places. A river bank, a pond, a garden, whatever tranquil location you would enjoy is the thing to imagine as your starting point. You need to construct your special place, your refuge. The more details you put into it, the better defined it becomes, and the easier it will be for you to go there.

In the case of a temple, you may want to see a long, narrow, rectangular pond. At the foot of the reflecting pond where you stand is an arched arbor entry. White roses are climbing over the trellis, and you must pass through the trellis to enter the temple area. Lily pads float on the pond, and it is lined by white marble, with a walkway that goes along either side. You lift your eyes and see that directly in front of you, beyond the pond, is a raised marble dais. There are curved steps that lead up to a central circular platform, surrounded by a colonnade of white marble, and surmounted by a domed alabaster roof. In the middle of this structure is a seat, a tripod of smoking incense, and a tall, footed candlestick containing a single lit candle.

You walk under the trellis and along the pool to the structure, hearing the murmur of the water and the chittering of birds as you pass. Smell the clean, fresh air and the perfumes of the flowers and plants around this tranquil garden. Feel the coolness of the air and the warmth of the stone as you ascend the steps in bare feet. Sit in the chair and gaze out into the garden, over the

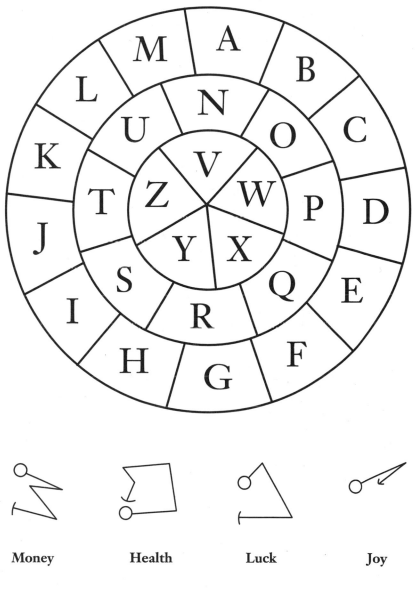

Money   **Health**   **Luck**   **Joy**

A Witch's Sigil Wheel

pond, at the gateway through which you have just passed. Now you look into the smoke of the incense and speak your word, or see your sigil. Listen and watch for the reply. When you have heard your answer, retrace the way you came, and return to ordinary consciousness.

Meditation in a personal circle.

To end the meditation, take a deep breath and exhale. Do so again, letting the meditation depart. Take a third breath, inhaling the sense of all being right in the world. Exhale and you are back in your meditation circle.

To open the circle, take your candlestick and walk around the ring in the opposite direction you walked to form it, addressing each Elemental as you go. In this case, you will now walk clockwise (deosil), starting at the North and moving to the East, South, and West, then returning to the North. At each Quarter, raise the candle as you give your farewell with open arms, and conclude with arms slightly crossed over your body, being careful with the candle flame. It is rather like a goodbye hug, and you say as your arms are open:

Farewell, Elemental (Air, Fire, Water, Earth)*!*

Then with arms closing:

Go in peace and my blessing take with you!

When you have farewelled the last Elemental, pinch out or snuff the candle and set it down. With the power tool used to create the circle, you now open it, North, to East, to South, to West, and back to North. See the light returning to you through the tool and passing back into the Earth. Say as you walk:

The circle is opened yet remains a circle as The Power flows in me and through me.

Touch the tool to your mid-forehead to seal the energy, ground yourself to drain the excess energy, and then have something to eat and drink.

Class 4
Review; Divinations; Assignment

Review

Rules of Conduct

- Be careful what you do
- Be careful who you trust
- Do not use The Power to hurt another because what is sent comes back
- Never use The Power against someone else who has The Power
- To use The Power you must feel it in your heart and know it in your mind

Divination

Divination Tools

The main purpose of divination in general is not to "predict" the future, but to see how the energies affecting future events are aligned so that you can either let things flow as they are or make changes to alter that alignment. Nothing is predestined in witchcraft because The Power of the Craft comes from the ability of the witch to create changes. Thus, if you see something you don't like, you can perform magics and call upon The Power to nudge the energies to a more agreeable or acceptable future. Sometimes the changes you are making will be for yourself, to assist in passing through a difficult time with less trauma than if you had been unprepared. At other times, you may want a clean slate. Choice is always involved here.

There are a number of tools that can be used for divination, but it is not necessary to expend a lot of money for these tools. Crystal ball scrying is typically thought of in connection with witchcraft, but a pan or bowl of water works equally well for scrying. Divination can take place in fire, smoke, cloud shapes and movement, bird flight, and the patterns of falling leaves. Anything connected with nature, if it inspires a feeling of meaningfulness within you, is a possible avenue for divination.

As I observed in *Green Witchcraft* (the text), visions can occur anywhere; if the Lady and the Lord want to show you something, they can give you a vision in your cereal bowl. It sounds facetious, but it is true. As an experiment, I once asked at breakfast for a vision that I would recognize of something ordinary from the day to come. I was stirring my coffee at the time, removed the spoon, and looked at the swirling cream. The image that formed was of an upside-down single rose with a long stem. My feeling was that this was not a portent or symbol so much as a marker—something to look for. That afternoon I was at a favorite shop chatting with the cashier as usual when something caught my eye. Behind her, she had, for no reason at all, that day pinned to the wall a single, long-stemmed rose—upside down. In my morning coffee cup I received what I had asked for—confirmation that visions can be found anywhere.

Scrying the clouds works on different levels of divination. Sometimes the clouds may show events to come, but usually the shapes and running movements resonate on an interior level. If you see a wild and reckless "rade" of horses and riders flying across the sky, you are getting a glimpse of the Wild Hunt and warning of turmoil in the place toward which the clouds are heading. If you see white unicorns, you have good fortune and success with you. If you see black unicorns, call upon the white unicorns to chase them away from where you are, for these are emotional storms and portents of disruptions in your life.

When invoking the Goddess at an Esbat, you will often see her form or face appear in the clouds around the Moon. Look for portents in the formation of clouds during unusual planetary events such as lunar and solar eclipses. You can also check the clouds for replies to your spell workings and invocations.

Tools for divination—a crystal ball, a bowl of water, tarot cards, and stones—or you might scan the clouds.

For divination in cards, a regular playing deck can be used with as much success as a tarot deck. The point of divination tools is not that they themselves hold a magical power, but that the diviner is able to focus through the tool.

A variety of small stones can be used as cards for divination if you pick up ones that provide you with distinct impressions. You could keep the pebbles in a bag and, when doing a divination, pull some out in a reading pattern (see text pages 119 and 121 for two examples). I have a collection of agates and rocks with natural images in them or shapes evocative of things of nature. One clear green stone has a black image of a figure like the Willendorf Mother Goddess in the center. Another has the image of a hare, another is in the shape of a heart, and so forth. When you gather your stones, you should meditate on each one in a quiet time with a white candle and a gentle incense to open your reception to the meaning of the stone. Once you see what a stone is, name your stone, and write down the name along with the meaning.

In time, a repeatedly used tool will gather energy and will work more quickly. You will find with cards, for example, that written meanings may not match what you are sensing from an arrangement, and this means that you are linking intuitively with the universe. Go with what this link tells you, rather than limiting yourself to the rote meanings of a tarot deck. As the tool absorbs your energies, it will respond more quickly to your inquiries and become tied to your energy fields. This does not color the reading; it makes the reading immediate. Although some people advise against reading your own cards, I disagree. A good reader will see the meanings in cards someone else reads for them, anyway. Your own interpretation is likely to be far more meaningful in such instances than someone else's.

Because of the energy alignments, you should not let other people handle or use your tools unless you hope to gain some benefit from this. There are times you may want someone with strong energy fields to handle something for you, with the objective of adding their energy to your own to enhance the power of the tool. This is rather like a "laying on of hands" and is only done in a positive manner with the energy directed to your aid. As tools gather attunement to you, the careless handling of your objects by other people could be detrimental by the addition of their own energies—sometimes in a great burst if excited about touching something "magical." This has the affect of diffusing or confusing the energies you have so carefully placed within.

When you have a tool that has been given an energy rush from someone else, you should cleanse it. You can follow the procedure on page 173 of the text for "Consecration of a Tool," or you can wash the tool in running water. If it is not practical to do this—as with a deck of cards, for example—you could pass the deck through incense, sprinkle it with spring water, wrap it in a white cloth, and bury it in clean soil for three days during the waning moon, to dissipate undesired energies. If a tool is washed, then do the consecration with salt (or burdock root), smoke, fire, and spring water. If the moon phase is waxing, recompose your reasoning accordingly: "to gain cleansing." With the waning moon, the reasoning is: "to dissipate the negative or extraneous energies."

Many people find tools for their Craft at antique shops, thrift stores, and garage sales. If you gain a tool this way, there might be unpleasant energies attached to it from the previous owners, neglect, or proximity to some other negatively charged item. When an object has particularly negative energies about it, another technique is to soak it. You would use sanctified water as a soak for the tool during a Full Moon (that is why it is a good idea to consecrate more than you need at an Esbat or a Sabbat and keep it bottled away from sunlight for later use). Let the item sit in this water under the rays of the Full Moon, then dry it off and bury it in soil from the Full to Dark Moon. Unbury it at the New Moon (when the first crescent shows) and wrap it in a white cloth. At the next Full Moon, consecrate the item.

On text pages 105–108, there is a list of symbols common to divinations. When you look at tea leaves, smoke, bird flight, clouds, and so forth, and see a symbol in them, you can check these pages for help in interpretation of their meanings. Often, the meaning will impress itself upon you at the time of sighting—but if not, these symbols may be used as a guide for similar symbols as well as those listed.

Crystal Ball Scrying

Genuine crystal balls are immensely expensive. The best source for them is Germany, where clear rock crystal has been mined and shaped for centuries. Other options that are less expensive are polished stones and balls made, like fine glassware, out of lead crystal. Large lead crystal balls can be found in various colors and often contain bubbles. These internal bubbles can aid in focusing, so that the visions that appear are inside the ball moving across a bubble. Although the materials are different, and crystal is the best natural energy source, visions can be drawn from anything if you are visual in your divinations.

The key to crystal ball, as well as mirror, scrying is to relax. Do not try to force a vision, do not strain yourself trying to see something. Visions come very gently and subtly. I recommend a quiet setting, or one with soothing music played very low. A candle and incense on either side of the crystal ball aid in your focus.

Look into the ball, try to find the center, and focus on that. If there is a bubble in the ball, this makes it easier to find a portion of the ball to focus on. Do not let your vision fuzz over. The objective is clear sight. It is okay to blink, just retain your focus. Soon the crystal ball will seem to be clouding inside.

Once you see the clouding of the ball, you have several options. If you want to ask about something in particular, whisper that question now and watch to see what unfolds. If you want to see something going on at the present time, whisper that question and watch. These two examples will generally result at first in a kind of silent movie in your focal point. What you are really doing is extending your awareness. With practice you will start to pick up on sounds, smells, and other sensations.

Another option when the ball clouds is to travel to another world. If this is what you want to do, be prepared for the journey. I have had students tell me that while crystal scrying, they felt they were falling inside, and had to have someone else "snap them out of it." Well, that is rather like going to the train station, putting your luggage on board, getting on, and when the conductor punches your ticket, jumping off the train and back to the platform. This simply means that you were not ready to travel. If you are afraid of travel, then do not try to push yourself into it.

If you desire to travel, then do so. I have had some marvelous experiences "falling" into Underworld, Otherworld, and so forth. The difference between making inquiries, seeing current or future events, and traveling is that you do not move with the first two. With the latter, however, you move within the crystal. What really happens is that the crystal expands and surrounds you.

When traveling to other worlds by the crystal ball, you will find that while you are alert and focusing on the center of the ball, the room around you becomes dimmer and dimmer until all you see is the crystal all around you. Retain your focus and you will travel. Jerk yourself out, and you return to where you began.

By moving into another world, you explore new realms and gain new perspectives and awarenesses. When your journey is done, you will return to where you started. The only thing you have to fear is your own fears. Traveling is sometimes one of the best ways to face your fears, expose them, understand them, and get past them. It is a very personal, spiritual, and cleansing experience.

Black Mirror Gazing

The black mirror is used in much the same way as the crystal ball. A black mirror can be purchased in New Age or occult supply stores and from catalogs (Appendix Two). These are also easy to make, and some of my students have created very artistic mirrors of their own. All you need is glass and black paint. A mirror functions by not letting light pass through the glass. Paint one side of a piece of glass in a shiny black, and then you may want to cover this side by gluing on a piece of black felt. You can get a framed glass such as is used for photos and treat the back of the glass the same way, return it to the frame, and have a framed black mirror. Some students have done this with round frames. You can also paint the black on aluminum foil and place the glass against the painted foil while it is still sticky, leaving perhaps a border of unpainted foil around the edge. You can inscribe pentacles, or whatever design you like, before placing the glass on it.

Some of the uses of the black mirror for meditations, travel, and spellwork are discussed in *Green Witchcraft II*, but the method of divination is the same as for the crystal ball. Gaze into the mirror and find the center. Then when the black mirror clouds with gray or white clouds, whisper your query and see what the response is. The Companion Quest utilizing a black mirror is described in the above book, and is best performed on the second dark moon of a solar month (calendar month). A companion becomes a guide, teacher, friend, and mentor from another world only if mutually agreeable to the parties involved.

In my classes, I have cautioned students not to use the Companion Quest, wherein you invite a spirit or entity to come close to you, unless seriously desiring one. Some have done so with success and seem quite pleased with the result. It is a matter of how comfortable you feel about having an "invisible" presence that makes itself known. For me, it is a matter of course, since spirit beings were always around us as I was growing up. Talking to "thin air" and having objects move on their own was normal in my home. We knew who our companions were and found their presence reassuring. I once saw a movie titled "High Spirits" in which I found amazing and amusing the way the film family interacted with spirits. It was like my own childhood home—talking to departed loved ones, being able to depend on spirit entities for help, and so forth.

Pendulum

The pendulum can be made from any weight that is suspended from a cord you hold in your hand. There are crystal and metal pendulums, suspended from fine chains or silk cords, but buttons or stones on a string or thread work as well. So once again, you do not need to purchase anything, only use what is at hand and in Nature. The essence of Green Witchcraft is the use of natural materials, for these have easily accessed energies.

You hold the pendulum between the thumb and forefinger of your *power hand* (the hand you favor), and sit with your elbow resting on a solid surface. Let the cord hang so it is unobstructed—not touching your arm or anything else. The pendulum should not touch the surface, but dangle above it. Relax and focus your sight into the center of the pendulum. If the pendulum is moving, say: "Be still," and focus that thought into the center of the pendulum. It will stop, and then you can start asking yes/no questions of it.

The first question you ask is one you know the answer to. Make it something very simple: "Did I drink coffee this morning?" or "Do I have red hair?" Watch the motion made by the pendulum. There are really two basic movements, linear and circular, and I have found that these vary with the individual asking the question. The motion that matches the correct answer to your starting question will continue to be the motion for that response—as long as *you* are asking the question. For me, circular is yes, linear is no, but for my daughter, it is the opposite. Curiously, I have a "negative" blood type, and she has a "positive" blood type, so I offer the speculation that there may be a connection between the positive/negative blood types and the circular/linear response for yes. But no matter what the blood characteristics, you will find a definite yes/no pattern in the movement of the pendulum.

Once you have established what is yes and what is no for you, you may ask any yes-no question and get a response. If the motion is slow, then the answer being given is not a definite one. It could change with different circumstances or influences. If the motion is rapid, then the stage is well set already and the energies are strongly disposed to that response. To alter that kind of prediction is harder than to nudge the slow-motion reaction. This may be a situation where you will want to prepare yourself for what is coming (be it beneficial or not, from your perspective) or try to blunt the impact, rather than throwing a lot of energy into attempting a total change of such a future.

The best way to go about change, should that be your decision, is to think about alternatives. This may require some meditation on your part to come up with new solutions or new directions you would like to take. Once you have several ideas, go back to the pendulum and address each idea as a possible means of making changes. If the pendulum responds enthusiastically to one of these ideas, then that would be the direction to take. If it is sluggish to all the ideas, then perhaps you should be considering internal changes rather than external ones. Divination tools are used for guidance and advice. How you respond is an individual decision.

When using the pendulum with other people, there are two methods from which to choose. One way is for you to ask the person's question, and the other is to let the other person ask the question. I prefer the first method since it avoids confusing the energies. If the other person asks, you again have to determine what is yes and what is no for that individual, which may be different from what is yes and no for you. This is when the problem of conflicting energies becomes evident. For consistency, I recommend the person tell you what they want to know, and you phrase and ask the question: "Will Sharon get a pay raise this month?" for example.

Tea Leaves

To read tea leaves, use loose leaf tea, rather than tea bags, generally one teaspoon per cup, and "one for the pot." This charming tradition can be thought of as giving a gift to receive a gift from the Elemental powers. Tea leaves are an easy divination technique because the energies of the individual and of the tea leaves are united in the process of holding the teacup and drinking the beverage.

Black teas are good for strong energies and general readings. These teas would include such types as English or Irish Breakfast teas, Earl Grey, and China Rose. Herbal teas are also excellent, and you can match the herb with the type of reading (check under the herb tab of your text). I like to use black tea as a base for herbal teas in magical practice. The black teas add magical power.

On textbook pages 113–114 several tea blends are suggested. For my classes, I like to prepare tea and pour a cup for everyone. The flavors are distinctive, and Fairy Tea seems quite popular. The recipe and the chant used in the making of this tea are not in *Green Witchcraft*, but are on pages 80–81 of the *Llewellyn 1997 Magical Almanac*:

3	tsp	English Breakfast Tea
$\frac{1}{2}$	tsp	chamomile
1	tsp	dandelion root
$1\frac{1}{2}$	tsp	elder flower
$1\frac{1}{2}$	tsp	hops
$1\frac{1}{2}$	tsp	mullein
$\frac{1}{2}$	tsp	raspberry leaf
$1\frac{1}{2}$	tsp	rose hips

As you place these ingredients into the teapot, chant:

Black for strength, then apple of night, wild grown root, and Lady's blessing. Leap for joy, then between the worlds, tangle of bramble and fairy love knots. Brewed to invite the fair folk to tea, working together, they and me.

This is the same recipe I recommend for the "Companion Quest Ritual" in *Green Witchcraft II*. A lot of the herbal teas are now available in the grocery store, but they can also be found or ordered at health food and nutrition stores. You can buy herbs in bulk or in teabags. One teabag equals one teaspoon, so you can snip open the bags if you want a more accurate measurement.

Once you have enjoyed your tea (you can still use milk and sweetener if you like) and only a small amount remains in your cup, you are ready for the divination. Take the teacup into your power hand and swirl the last bit of tea around clockwise three times. Let the tea leaves settle into place as you rest the cup in the opposite hand. I give an example of a divination chant on text page 110 to use while swirling the tea.

Look at the leaves and see what images come to mind. Do not strain at this—simply go with the first impressions. A reading can be very brief or more complicated, depending on the amount of tea leaves in the cup and the patterning resulting from being swirled. If one major image appears to you, then check it against those listed under the tab, "Symbols" (text pages 105–108). As ever with divinations, your intuition is the best guide for your readings. Learn to open yourself to receive the impressions through relaxation and connection to the Elemental powers. I have found at times that very complex images appear, in which a scenario is impressed upon me. Changes in the workplace, influences of other people, and so forth can appear in the leaves. You are letting the leaves act as your focus for the divination, and the visual images may include more than simply tea leaf formations.

Class 4

Tarot

There are numerous tarot decks available today, or for divination, a regular deck of playing cards will work equally well. As is usual for divination, the cards show how things stand at the present time, and how things *may* proceed if left unattended. If events are too far along to be altered substantially, the cards can offer guidance for dealing with upcoming situations or taking evasive action. The text gives suggested interpretations for tarot cards on pages 122–126, but the meanings may vary depending upon the deck used. In a listing for tarot meanings, pick the one that feels most appropriate to you, based upon the surrounding cards, the matter being discussed, and the deck itself.

Although I have listed reverse meanings, I only use these when I sense they are pertinent, and I know there are others who view the tarot in the same way. I see the tarot as having sufficient cards to cover all the bases upright, so that The Power will select the necessary cards for a reading. The cards will not get into a reversed position unless they are scattered and stirred around on a table-top. I prefer to have them all upright, and after the person for whom I am doing the reading has knocked on the deck, and I have proclaimed it that person's deck, I shuffle, cut, and lay out the spread. If a subject wants a more thorough investigation into one aspect of a reading, then I will spread the deck out face down on the table and move the cards around. The subject may then draw out the cards for the reading.

Tarot illustrations have an influence on the meanings, and you will find your interpretations will vary by deck and by reading. In some decks, the 10 of swords is nightmarish, and I use this card along with the Devil card to judge whether or not a deck is one I can use. The 10 of swords is a card that some diviners see as a card of disaster, but there are many decks that see this card as one of turning your back on a bad situation and moving on. I prefer this interpretation, because 10 is a very positive number in divination, a number for success and completion, while swords refer to the intellect. This card represents, then, a struggle of intellect and mindset where a person has finally determined there is no point in continuing with a currently hurtful thought pattern, and turns away from that to a more positive tomorrow.

For the Craft, there is no such being as the devil. Some decks use other terms for the intent of this card—the Horned God for natural blessings or things taking their natural course. It can show a person will be pulled in different directions until a decision is made. It can also depict the desire for and the lure of material possessions, and warns a person to not let that be the whole of one's endeavors. Mostly, the "Devil" is the allure of chaos, wild Nature, and unihibited freedom. It is also revelry and the harvest celebration.

What are usually called Major and Minor Arcana in tarot, I see as Arcane cards of universal influence (mystical archetypes), Power cards of Elemental influences (Aces), Mundane cards of life experiences (2–10), and Royal cards of people or personal characteristics (Page, Knight, Queen, King). Arcane cards are normally read right-side up, and Power cards always are. You will find that your interpretations for cards will change as you gain more experience, and you will be drawn to certain tarot decks. I like to vary the decks I use with the season, the moon phase, the Sabbat, and the purpose of the reading. Most witches end up having a number of tarot decks, but playing cards may also be used. In this case, one particular deck should be used only for divination.

With playing cards, the interpretations are a little different. There is no major arcana, and in the minor arcana, the page/ princess card is combined with the knight to become the jack. A jack in a regular playing deck can mean news, young people, and thoughts taking direction or moving into action. The meanings for the rest of the playing cards can be seen as the same as with tarot, or slightly altered. The suits are more generalized. Hearts are love and emotions; diamonds are money and success; clubs are career and social matters; and spades are more often related to difficulties, illnesses, and warnings.

Aces remain as power cards. Two aces imply a marriage, three to four show great success. Multiple queens may warn of gossip or scandal, unless you can see individuals in these cards and identify a connection to the querant. Multiple kings suggest big business dealings, while multiple jacks suggest mischief or competition. Three or more 10s show something good on the horizon, possibly more money, while three or more 9s suggest sudden good fortune. The 9 of hearts is considered a "wish" card—make a wish when you see it, and it will come true.

The throws also affect the interpretation of card readings. Two sample tarot spreads are shown on text pages 119 (Tree of Life) and 121 (Celtic Cross). For a quick read, there is also the five-card Elemental Spread shown below. Ask a question as you shuffle the deck. Set the cards down, cut the deck and restack. Pull the first card as you say, "This is the answer by Earth," and lay the card face up in the North position (top of the reading area). Pull the second card as you say, "By Air," and set it face up at the East (to your right). Pull the third card and say, "By Fire," and set it face up at the South (at the bottom of the reading area). Pull the fourth card and say, "By Water," and set it face up at the West (to your left). Pull the fifth card and say, "And by Spirit this answers all," and set it face up in the center. You

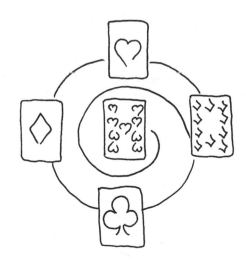

Five Card Elemental Tarot spread.

75

should now have what looks like a modified Celtic Cross with this spread.

The Earth card should be read as physical influences on the question, the Air card as mental influences, the Fire card as energy influences, and the Water card as emotional influences. The center Spirit card is the answer to the question.

This spread can be altered by first setting the five cards around face down as you say: "This is the hidden influence of Earth," etc. Then go around again laying the next set of five cards face up as described above. Once you see your quick reply, you can then turn over the hidden influences in each of these realms. The hidden influences motivate or push the more apparent influences to your answer.

Another easy spread for a quick response, when you are unsure what to ask, is the Situation Spread. Shuffle, cut, and re-stack the deck, then lay out the seven cards left to right, face up with the first three in one row, the fourth in the center, and the fifth to seventh cards in a row below the fourth card. It looks a little like an hour glass. In the top row, card 1 is the past, card 2 is the present, card 3 is the future. The center position is card 4, and this tells you what is really on your mind. It might re-state your query, or it might show some underlying concern. On the bottom row, moving left to right, card 5 shows the attitude of someone else who is involved. Sometimes there is not another person involved and the meaning may relate to the querant's attitude or to other influences. Card 6 shows obstacles, if any, and card 7 shows the likely outcome to the situation.

Runes

The last divination tool I want to discuss here is the runes. In the text pages 102–103, there are meanings listed for various runes, but these are aimed at inscriptions for magical practices, such as with candle magics. You can either buy a set of runes (some come with their own book of interpretations) or make your own. To make a set of 25 runes, you can paint the symbols on pebbles, chips of wood, tile squares, and even engrave them on crystals and pieces of metal. The first example is the easiest.

Keep your runes in a cloth bag, and consecrate them to your use as you would any tool. When not in use, store them in the bag in a box or a drawer, so they do not pick up a lot of extraneous energies. As with most tools, you should not let other people handle them. For other people to get readings from you, leave the runes in their bag and let the person hold the bag while concentrating on a query. Then take the bag from the person, open it, and draw out the runes, laying them in a spread as you go.

The following guide is for divination with runes. First is the rune, then the name of the rune, the meaning of the rune, and finally some additional interpretations of the rune.

ᛗ Mannuz = Self: self-improvement, cooperation, moderation, thoughts

ᚷ Gefu = Gifts/Partnership: union, settlements, equity, gifts

ᚠ As = Wisdom/Signals: occult power, healing, awareness

ᛉ Ethel = Possessions/Home: heritage, benefits, new path, gains

ᚢ Uruz = Strength: health, promotion, changes, passage

ᛈ Perth = Destiny: opportunity, good fortune, secrets revealed

ᚾ Nyo = Constraint/Patience: self-control, obstacles overcome

ᛝ Ing = Fertility: potential, goals achievable, completion

ᛇ Eoh = Channel/Defense: energy motion, psychic communication

ᛉ Elhaz = Protection/Friendship: aspirations, optimism, aid

ᚩ Feoh = Prosperity: fulfillment, satisfaction, wealth

ᚹ Wyn = Joy/Comfort: harmony, success, well-being

⟨ Gera = Harvest: tangible results, good outcome in time, cycle

⟨ Ken = Opening/Energy: fresh start, positivity, new freedom

↑ Tyr = Victory: success, courage, favorable outcome to action

Β Beorc = Growth: ideas manifested, gentle action, family

Μ Eh = Progress/Movement: swift changes to secure position

Γ Lagu = Fluidity/Emotions: psychic powers, vitality, review

Η Haegal = Limits/Disruptions: break from constrictive ideas

Ρ Rad = Journey/Quest: safe journey, attunement, seek and find

Þ Thorn = Protection/Gateway: safety, foes neutralized, defense

Μ Daeg = Breakthrough/Ambition: catalyst, transformation

Ι Is = Stasis/Standstill: rest, refocus, pause in activity

Ϟ Sigel = Wholeness/Achievement: vitality, healing, power

Ο Wyrd = Fate/Destiny: total trust, cosmic power, self-change

Runes may be seen as relating to the major arcana of the tarot, with the Wyrd being equated to the Fool, who comes at the start or finish of the tarot, depending on the circumstances. See if you can make your own list matching major arcana with the runes.

There are several runic spreads you may want to practice with. The first type uses three runes drawn from the bag and laid out in a line, left to right, to advise you on the direction a query may go. The first rune shows the present situation, the second shows the action needed for the query, and the third rune offers a possible result.

A simple yes/no question can be answered by pulling out three runes. If they all come out with the symbol right side up, the answer is yes. If they all come out with the symbol upside down, the answer is no. If they are mixed, the results could go either way.

With a runic cross, you use six runes placed (1) top, (2) left, (3) bottom, (4) below bottom, (5) right, and (6) center. 1 is the past and past influences; 2 is the present and present influences; 3 is the future and future influences; 4 is the foundation for these influences in the situation/question; 5 shows the possible obstacles to achieving a goal; and 6 shows what situations are on the horizon.

Another runic throw uses five runes in the style of the Elemental Cross tarot reading to address a particular situation. The first rune is laid at the top of the spread (North) and offers an overview of the situation. The second rune is laid at the right side (East) and shows possible challenges to the situation. The third rune lays at the bottom of the spread (South) and suggests action needed to gain the desired goal. The fourth rune goes on the left side (West) and provides a look at some options or choices related to this situation. The fifth rune is laid at the center (Spirit) and shows the outcome, or how the situation is likely to turn out.

Assignment

1. Review chapters five and six of *Green Witchcraft*.

2. Try some divination techniques yourself. Do a relaxing meditation first, then move into the divination. Record your readings.

3. Answer the following questions:

   a. How do you find North?

   _____

   b. What are three kinds of creative meditations?

       1._____

       2._____

       3._____

c. Name five divination tools.

1._____ 2._____ 3._____

4._____ 5._____

d. State a Green Witchcraft intent and a focus for meditation:

Intent:_____

Focus :_____

e. What are two purposes for meditation?

1._____

2._____

Answers to Questions

3a. Find where the sun rises (East) and sets (West)—to face North, in the morning put the sun at your right shoulder, in the afternoon at your left shoulder.

3b. Spontaneous song; speaking in tongues; automatic writing/ poetry.

3c. Crystal ball; pendulum; tea leaves; cards; runes; mirror; clouds.

3d. Intents: healing; oneness; spiritual guide
Focuses: union; identity; communication

3e. Here you could answer: connecting with the various aspects of the earth and universe; accessing the subconscious mind to solve problems; enhancing learning ability; promoting good health by mental relaxation, and calming the nervous system; open creative awareness; journey to other worlds/planes.

Class 5

Review; Divination
with the Celtic Ogham;
Assignment

Review

Rules of Conduct

Without going back into the last lesson or the textbook, see if you can recite the five Rules of Conduct. Turn to page 8 of the first class and look at the list. Did you miss any? If so, softly repeat the rules two or three times aloud so you can hear the words as well as see them. Consider how the Rules apply to your practice of the Craft.

Set Up an Altar/Working Area

Since I set up a different altar with each class, you might want to try one now that is unlike whatever you have been previously using. Some options for deity images for altars besides statuary are with deity candles—blue for the Lady, orange or yellow for the Lord. These can be votive size, pillar variety, or tapers in candlestick holders. Another altar option is with stones—round for the Lady, long for the Lord—or a shell for the Lady, and a pine cone for the Lord; flower for the Lady, and seed for the Lord. These are fairly standard motifs for the Goddess and the God.

Light a candle before the images and an incense such as sage for learning. Choose the candle color from the listing on page 63–64 of the text. Some good choices would be amber, gold, yellow, indigo, purple, or white.

Cast the Learning Circle

If you want to proceed with other ritual items, by all means do so, otherwise you are ready to cast a simple circle. Sweep the area deosil with besom or leaves:

> *As I sweep, may the besom chase away all negativity from within this circle that it may be cleared and ready for my work.*

Then clap your hands three times and state:

> *The circle is about to be cast and I freely stand within to work and learn in this class.*

Move around the circle with the tool of your choice (athame, wand, or your hand) to draw the circle, envisioning the blue light:

> *I draw this circle around me, through walls and floors, above me and below me, as a sphere is the circle cast in the presence of the powers of Earth, Air, Fire, and Water* (the Lady and the Lord) *that they may aid and bless me in my studies.*

Return the tool to the altar. With arms upraised in greeting, say:

> *The circle is cast and consecrated to the powers of Nature and the universe. Only love shall enter and leave.*

The Elementals may be called upon at the quarters if you like, but this style of casting calls the Elementals without going to the North, East, South, and West of the circle for separate invocations.

You are ready to work inside your circle. When you are finished, you simply open the circle by announcing the conclusion of your work, giving your blessings to the Lady and the Lord (if you use a deity format) and to the Elementals. Then you call their blessings upon yourself, and bid farewell to the Elementals, and to any visiting beings, visible and invisible:

> *My blessings take with thee; Thy blessings upon me,*
> *for we are kith kin, thee and me. Depart in peace*
> *Elementals Earth, Air, Fire, Water. Depart in peace,*
> *beings visible and invisible; my blessings take with*
> *you. The circle is opened.*

Go around the circle withdrawing back into the tool and into yourself the blue light that you used to create the circle, then ground the excess energy. Tidy up the work area, extinguish the candles, and take some refreshment before resuming your usual routine.

Ogham

Three Worlds and the Midhe

A deeper exploration of the Ogham may be found in chapter 6 of *Green Witchcraft*, as is the listing of meanings for the fews in each world and realm shown here. The Ogham is unique in that it presents a three-dimensional reading. I have seen books in which this is alluded to, with the dimensions being stated, but inevitably, the throws are rather much like tarot or runic throws. My method moves the diviner into the realms according to how the fews land. The sequence of my listing matches the casting as a witch's circle: North, East, South, and West, but Robert Graves' *The White Goddess* (page 115) lists by North, West, East, South. There is no hard, fast rule so you can be flexible.

The three worlds of the ogham are Middleworld—the world of physical existence; Underworld—the world of the afterlife, or Shadowland; and Otherworld—the world of higher spiritual development. Each world has four quarters, called realms, which are the North, the East, the South, and the West. The centerpoint of each world where the quarters meet is the midhe, the focus or midpoint (middle).

The quarters are represented by the Three Queens and their King, or the Triple Goddess and the God who passes through three phases (son, husband, perfect sacrifice).

The God of Witchcraft is the King of the South, the sun who moves through the solar phases. He is newborn at winter solstice (the Sabbat of Yule) and rules as the lord of the wildwood and of animals (through the Sabbat of Litha, or Midsummer Eve). When the God becomes the husband of the Goddess (the Sabbat of Lughnassadh is also called the Marriage of Lugh, the Celtic name of the Sun God), he gives his life energy into the Goddess as Earth to grow the crops that feed the animals and humanity. By sacrificing himself into her, he also impregnates her with himself (hence the Sabbat of Mabon). He then rules the Underworld as Lord of Shadows (during the Sabbat of Samhain) until reborn at winter solstice. This is the unending spiral dance of life, passage, and rebirth celebrated in the Old Religion.

The Triple Goddess is the Lady as Maiden (Queen of the West), Mother (Queen of the East), and Crone (Queen of the North).

North symbolizes the realm of the Crone or Hag; the Snow Queen; and Winter. Here are generated the conflicts and frictions that drive us into taking action. This realm offers both the creative spur and the obstacles of life, but I see these as motivators. You can turn around a negative or challenging situation to power up a response, or to learn and grow. Challenges are what the mind needs to expand knowledge, be inventive, and overcome obstacles. In this manner, the self-confidence grows and the spirit brightens with new capabilities.

East symbolizes the realm of the Earth Mother; the Great Mother; and Autumn. It is a place of opportunities and fertility. This is the realm of bounty and harvest symbolized by the grid of a ploughed field. Here what you have sown is reaped in material manifestation.

South symbolizes the realm of the Lord of the Sun; the Greenman. The energy of Summer's sun offers harmony in this quarter, a place where foundations are laid and the harmonious influences in the reading may be found.

West symbolizes the realm of learning belonging to the Lady of the West, who is also Sophia, the Lady of Wisdom. Here are found the Spring of learning and one's intellectual development. Fews in this quarter show a person's mental and spiritual state of being.

The seasons need not be applied in readings, and there may be other interpretations of the seasonal rotation. The movement I have described presents the oppositions of solstices and equinoxes, giving the casting cloth a connection to the Quarter Sabbats.

There is one more place indicated in the ogham divination spread—the center point. The focus of the reading lays at this center point, and it is also where you will find the symbolic point of passage from one world to another. The reading begins with the few closest to the center point.

Each world has the same four realms and the midhe (center point), but the interpretations vary for the quarters according to the world in which they lie. The names of the realms are usually described as *forfedha*, additional letters, with IO for the North; AE for the East; OI for the South; UI for the West; and EA for the Midpoint (Midhe). Because these were later additions to the ogham, there is a sense of forfeit—a taking away from the secrecy of the original alphabet of divination, hence a revealing of the hidden realms. The ogham is multi-layered in both letters and meanings, as I hope to show, and this is what makes divination by ogham a potentially powerful system, if you have the patience to learn it. Do not be afraid of developing notes to read by, because until you gain familiarity with the system, it can be difficult to remember the interrelationships of the meanings. Here are the names of the realms that lie in each world:

The North is called the realm of Cath—this is symbolized by two superimposed Xs (⬭), and represents Friction.

The East is called the realm of Blath—this is symbolized by a grid (⬭), and represents Harvest.

The South is called the realm of Seis—this is symbolized by two triangles placed base to base (◇), and represents Balance.

The West is called the realm of Fis—this is symbolized by a spiral curl (⟋⟲), and represents Enlightenment.

The Center is called Midhe—this is symbolized by the X of the center of the casting cloth, and represents the Focus.

The 21 Fews

The *fews* are the letters of the Celtic Tree Alphabet, named for trees, shrubs, and vines, and representing hidden meanings. Robert Graves sees the order of the letters as reflecting changes in religious focus, yet his arrangement of the letters coincides with my own except that we hold the North and South fews in reverse. My listing shows the one-tine fews in the first group, followed by the twos, and so forth. You may want to try different placements with a group, but then be consistent throughout the rest of the groups.

The three worlds each have four letters representing each realm. Between the worlds are the letters that represent the paths leading to and from those worlds, through the midhes. You have a three dimensional layer of worlds, then, with four fews acting as connecting paths between Otherworld and Middleworld, and four fews acting as connecting paths between Middleworld and Underworld. Each world-realm has a meaning, and the realms and paths are each represented by a letter with a meaning:

Otherworld: N ᚔ Age: Iodho-yew (I) transformation/ immortality

E ᚏ Abundance: Ruis-elder (R) evolution/ new paths

S ᚅ Happiness: Nion-ash (N) awakening/ rebirth

W ᚊ Light: Quert-apple (Q) regeneration/ perfection

Paths:

1. ᚓ Eadha-aspen (E)—intuition/gains
2. ᚄ Saille-willow (S)—psychic power
3. ᚎ Straif-blackthorn (Z)—destruction
4. ᚉ Coll-hazel (C)—wisdom/creativity

Middleworld: N ᚒ Challenge: Ur-heather (U) fervor/gateway

E ᚍ Prosperity: Ngetal-reed (Ng) inner transformation

S ᚃ Contentment: Fearn-alder (F) awareness/ inner power

W ᚈ Knowledge: Tinne-holly (T) tests/ choices/balance

Paths:

1. ᚑ Onn-gorse (O)—opportunity/changes
2. ᚂ Luis-rowan (L)—foresight/healing
3. ᚌ Gort-ivy (G)—tenacity/skills
4. ᚇ Duir-oak (D)—truth/endurance

Underworld: N ᚐ Endings: Ailm-fir (A)—discretion/serenity

E ᚋ Growth: Muin-vine (M)—fruition/ introspection

S ᚁ Energy: Beithe-birch (B) beginnings/ forces of growth

W ᚆ Love: Huath-hawthorn (H) cleansing/ pleasure

Blank | Destiny: wyrd-mistletoe—fate/hidden cosmic influences

The blank few influences the area in which it lands. The world and realm read for the blank is determined by whether or not there are path fews in that quarter.

Casting Cloth

The casting cloth used in ogham divination is a flat, square surface that is marked off as I will show in a moment. The creativity of the reader must come into play here, because when you look at this cloth, you have to recognize that you are actually looking at three worlds lying one on top of the other. The fews are the keys to passage and are the keys that turn the worlds, and the worlds turn around the central midhe—yourself. Mannuz in the runic symbology is the Self, and you are the center of your universe.

To use the ogham for divination and meditation, create a *casting cloth* symbolizing Middleworld by cutting out a large square, then sew or draw the large X on the square from corner to corner. Draw or sew a smaller square near the center of the cloth. Draw or sew the symbols of the Three Queens and the King on the line of the inner square that passes through the appropriate quarter: Cath, Blath, Seis, and Fis. The midhe, or Focal Point, is the "X" at the very center of the square (see illustration).

There are different styles of casting cloths, and depending on your sewing skill, you may come up with something quite spectacular. I have seen the cloth done up in a large, green double-sided square of fabric with silk cord drawstrings that encircle the cloth so that the whole can be drawn together as a large pouch. The four symbols of the quarters are embroidered on the inner lines. The fews, then, reside inside the pouch. My own casting cloth is outlined in rose-ribbons (the spooled craft ribbon with rosebuds fasioned along the length) of different colors representative of each quarter. The symbols are done in plain, colored ribbons. The cloth is folded and kept inside a pouch, along with the fews, and the pouch hangs on my stang.

You could use paper and pencil, or simply the dirt on the ground, etched with the squares and lines of the worlds. Although there are people who see earth solely for the grounding of energy, I consider the earth as also the fertile source of growth energy. Many times a circle is cast in the dust of the earth at a campsite, or in the sand of the beach, so why not use it for a casting cloth? What could make a better casting cloth than the surface of Mother Earth?

Interpretations

The twenty-one fews of the ogham may be losely associated with the twenty-one major arcana, but the Celtic sensations that move with the ogham are not necessarily the same as with the tarot or with runes. Ogham fews are *very* primal, and very Green in emphasis—the letters representing trees, shrubs, and vines. The ogham is not related to the medieval kabbalah tradition nor even completely to Northern runic symbolism. As such, any tarot comparisons that can be drawn are best when seen in non-kabbalic interpretations in such decks as the Old Path, Herbal, Cat People, Londa (which is *very* Elvin), and some of the decks based on alchemy (the art of turning metals into gold, and the earliest form of chemistry). This latter style of tarot deck is rarely found in a purely alchemical form. Most are handmade, and a delight to use for their earthy solidity of mineral, metal, and planetary relationships.

Each of the twenty-one fews has a meaning, but that meaning is influenced by the world and the realm in which it lands, resulting in variations. The key meaning of the few is the emphasis of the reading when there is a few directly on the midhe. This few will be the first one read, and the starting world for it is Middleworld. Therefore, rather than the fews simply having 21 meanings, there are an additional 252 shadings of these meanings dependent on where they land other than in midhe, for a total of 273 possible meanings.

As you can see, there is a lot of flexibility in this system of divination, especially when the throw is directed at a particular question. The answers tend to be very thorough. In the listing provided here, the meaning of the few is stated first, which is used when the few is in midhe; then the meaning is shaded by each world and each realm of each world. OW is Otherworld; MW is Middleworld; UW is Underworld. N, E, S, or W indicate the four quarters of the world in which the few lies in a given throw: for example, OW-N means Otherworld, Northern realm.

Before doing a throw, you should focus on a question or problem you want the ogham to address. I suggest formulating a question, and when you are through with the reading, arranging the response into a coherent sentence-style reply.

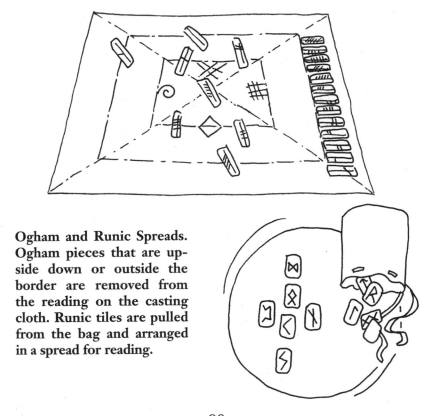

Ogham and Runic Spreads. Ogham pieces that are upside down or outside the border are removed from the reading on the casting cloth. Runic tiles are pulled from the bag and arranged in a spread for reading.

A Complete Listing for Ogham Interpretation*

1. ⌗ Transformation/Ends/Immortality

Iodho in:

OW-N: Age or wisdom brings an ending, transformation, immortality

OW-E: Ending of bounty or transformation into abundance

OW-S: Ending of one kind of happiness, change in joy

OW-W: Changed by light of inspiration or by gentleness

MW-N: Challenge motivates a change, brings immortality

MW-E: Reaping a small harvest; change in prosperity

MW-S: Contentment/harmony ends and interests change

MW-W: Transformed by new knowledge

UW-N: Period of significant endings and changes

UW-E: Youthfulness transformed by growth

UW-S: Life changes; end of one kind of life is transformed with new Energy into another; new vitality

UW-W: Transformation of love to immortality; end of a love

2. ⌗ Change/Evolution

Ruis in:

OW-N: Wisdom leads to new path; old ways decay; evolution into new forms

OW-E: Change in bounty; deterioration of delight pushes for new path

OW-S: Old forms of happiness replaced with new ones

OW-W: Lack of contentment inspires search for a new path; peace comes from releasing what is outmoded

MW-N: Challenge to old ways leads to new forms

MW-E: Gains deteriorate/not as great as expected; new methods needed for success

MW-S: Contentment/harmony comes in due course; that which brings satisfaction is in a state of change; seeking new goals

MW-W: Learning brings changes; knowledge results in evolution

---

* *Green Witchcraft II: Balancing Light and Shadow* (Llewellyn Publications, 1998)

UW-N: Old patterns give way to new ideas; need to adjust to changes

UW-E: Evolution and growth emphasized to maintain youthful outlook

UW-S: Old ways revitalized to produce a new perspective; change through energy

UW-W: New love coming; seeking new friends

3. ᛝ Awakening/Rebirth/Peace

Nion in:

OW-N: Awakening and communication of wisdom; new influence through age/longevity/tenure

OW-E: Abundance brings peace; fruitful communications; reward

OW-S: Happiness communicated; new joy in life

OW-W: Peace emphasized; inspiration and rebirth; hope

MW-N: Challenges open awareness; friction soothed by communication and influence; renewal of efforts

MW-E: Prosperity through communication; peaceful harvest

MW-S: New influence leads to harmony/contentment; awakening to the things that matter

MW-W: New awareness through learning; communication of knowledge; old knowledge reborn

UW-N: Awakening and rebirth changes endings to new beginnings and brings transformations into being

UW-E: Rebirth of youth; awakening of growing process; communication/new influence with youths

UW-S: revitalization; reenergized; vital communications; dynamic renewal of efforts

UW-W: Love/pleasure rediscovered; peace in relationships through communication; love as a new influence

4. ᛟ Regeneration/Eternity/Life

Quert in:

OW-N: Age or wisdom brings a regeneration or a new life

OW-E: Renewal of abundance

OW-S: Happiness from a new life; enjoyment of beauty

OW-W: New calmness in life; perfection in peacefulness

MW-N: Challenge leads to regeneration or a new life
MW-E: Return of prosperity; upturn in fortune; reap rewards
MW-S: Contentment from beauty/perfection; harmony in life
MW-W: Renewal/perfecting of knowledge
UW-N: Ending brings regeneration; perfection ideal changes
UW-E: Growth brings new youthfulness; eternally young
UW-S: Energy and life revitalized
UW-W: Love renewed; love of life, beauty, the arts

5. ╫ Intuition/Overcoming Obstacles (Path to Otherworld)

Eadha in:
OW-N: Sensitive to elders; wisdom gained through intuition
OW-E: Obstacles to abundance overcome; sharing of bounty
OW-S: Kindliness leads to happiness; follow instincts for bliss
OW-W: Inspiration by intuition; peace gained by perseverance
MW-N: Challenges overcome; intuition is accurate
MW-E: Obstacles overcome to gain prosperity; rewards from caring for others
MW-S: Intuition/sensitivity leads to harmony/contentment; obstacles to harmony overcome
MW-W: Knowledge comes intuitively; obstacles to learning overcome; sensitive use of knowledge
UW-N: Transformed by intuition; obstacles end
UW-E: Enjoyment of youth; intuition leads to growth
UW-S: Energy to overcome obstacles; strong intuition
UW-W: Sensitivity to others increases love and pleasure; follow intuition in matters of the heart

6. ╥ Intuition/Flexibility (Path to Otherworld)

Saille in:
OW-N: Wisdom enhanced by psychic power; liberation in age
OW-E: Abundance gives liberation; bounty through intuition
OW-S: Happiness comes from flexibility; intuition/psychic power brings bliss
OW-W: Flexibility for peace; intuition leads to inspiration
MW-N: Challenge to use psychic power wisely; friction eased by flexibility

MW-E: Prosperity from intuition and psychic power; what is sent comes back

MW-S: Use of intuition to find contentment; in harmony with psychic power; contentment from adaptability

MW-W: Flexibility in learning and knowledge; wide variety of interests; intuitive learning; liberation through knowledge

UW-N: Psychic power is transforming; end of restrictions

UW-E: Growth of intuition and psychic power

UW-S: Psychic energy; vitality of freedom; keenly intuitive

UW-W: Love is intuitive; adaptability in finding love and enjoyment; liberation in love; psychic power enhances love

7. ⚏ Coercion/Control Through Force (Path to Otherworld)

Straif in:

OW-N: Wisdom controlled by others; obstacles of age turned to benefits

OW-E: Abundance lacking; bounty dissipated

OW-S: Happiness muted by others; own joy lies in the hands of others

OW-W: Inspiration muted; peace enforced by others; dissatisfaction

MW-N: Challenged to seize control of own life; use destructive power against obstacles

MW-E: Prosperity controlled by others; obstacles to goals need to be overcome for independence and success

MW-S: Disharmony; discontent; need to break free of constraints to attain own contentment

MW-W: Learning is a difficult process; knowledge seems controlled and constricted; need to explore new ideas

UW-N: Destructive power turned against obstacles; ending of coercion; transformation of negative forces into positive ones

UW-E: Growth inhibited; control of youth

UW-S: Energy controlled by others; vitality dependent on others

UW-W: Forbearance in love; false pleasure; pretense of love; dominance in love can lead to its destruction; resignation to will of others in love/pleasure

8. ⅏ Wisdom/Creativity/Perception (Path to Otherworld)

Coll in:

OW-N: Strong wisdom; career in science/writing/creativity; mental power; understanding is accurate

OW-E: Bounty and abundance from wisdom and creative expression

OW-S: Understanding brings happiness; joy in writing/science

OW-W: Inspirational turn of mind; spiritual writing; perceptions for peacefulness

MW-N: Wisdom/understanding challenged; friction in creativity

MW-E: Prosperity from creativity/understanding

MW-S: Wisdom leads to harmony; contentment from creativity

MW-W: Educational writing; perceptive ability increases knowledge; participation in learning

UW-N: Transformation of wisdom; misunderstanding; perceptions change

UW-E: Wisdom grows; youthful audience; writing for young people; science endeavors beginning to grow; creativity and understanding increases

UW-S: Energy to pursue interests

UW-W: Love of learning; pleasure in creative efforts

9. ⚋ Fervor/Gateway/Success/Gains

Ur in:

OW-N: Wisdom provides a gateway to strong self-expression/ gains

OW-E: Success brings abundance

OW-S: Happiness through strong self-expression; gains bring bliss

OW-W: Inspirational fervor; peace from success

MW-N: Friction leads to strong self-expression; challenge brings success

MW-E: Highly successful; many gains; fervor and self-expression reap successful harvest

MW-S: Harmony from successes; strong self-expression moderated for contentment and gains

95

MW-W: Gains in knowledge/learning; self-expression in knowledge; philosopher; education is a gateway to success
UW-N: Self-expression is a gateway to transformation; gains dwindle and new forms for success need to be found
UW-E: Success is a gateway to growth; youthful self-expression
UW-S: Energy and fervor invigorate self-expression and gains
UW-W: Enjoyment of self-expression; pleasure from success; ardent in pursuit of love and pleasure

10. ᚍ Harmony/Inner Development

Ngetal in:
OW-N: Age/wisdom brings internal transformation/development
OW-E: Abundance comes from inner development
OW-S: Happiness lies in internal transformation
OW-W: Harmony from inspiration; peacefulness within
MW-N: Harmony difficult to maintain; inner development challenged; friction leads to internal transformation
MW-E: Balance is harvest of inner development
MW-S: Harmony/contentment emphasized through internal transformation
MW-W: Knowledge/learning has a profound, transformative affect
UW-N: Transformation emphasized through internal development and harmony; end of harmony through internal transformation
UW-E: Growth of harmony; youthful inner transformation; emphasis on inner development
UW-S: Energy for internal transformation/development; vitality for harmony
UW-W: Internal transformation/inner development through love; harmony in pleasure

11. ᚃ Inner Strength/Foundations

Fearn in:
OW-N: Wisdom emphasized as awareness ends doubts; inner strength through wisdom/age
OW-E: Foundation of abundance; awareness/appreciation of bounty; generosity

OW-S: Foundation of happiness; bliss from awareness/end of doubts; satisfaction

OW-W: Inspiration to inner strength; peace through end of doubt

MW-N: Friction leads to ending of doubts; challenge brings inner strength

MW-E: Prosperity from determination

MW-S: Contentment from awareness and end of doubts; harmony from inner strength

MW-W: Learning ends doubts; foundation of knowledge brings inner strength

UW-N: Awareness is transformative; ending of doubts emphasized; inner strength develops

UW-E: Growth of awareness to overcome doubts; youthful foundation of inner strength

UW-S: Vitality of inner strength; energy to open awareness

UW-W: Love faced with full awareness; inner strength brings pleasure; doubt-free love

12. ᛗ Balance/Retribution

Tinne in:

OW-N: Age and wisdom bring new challenges for balance

OW-E: Balance needed in decisions affecting bounty

OW-S: Choices to be made for happiness

OW-W: Peace through balance

MW-N: Challenges to balance mounting; retribution/justice; care needed in making decisions in time of friction

MW-E: Balance needed for prosperity; choices determine the harvest

MW-S: Contentment from balance; harmony affected by decisions

MW-W: Learning determined by conscious decisions; balanced education; tests of knowledge

UW-N: Endings from retribution; transformation to balance by decisions

UW-E: Balanced growth; tests in youth; decisions/choices affect growth

UW-S: Energy to maintain balance; vitality to overcome tests; choices approached with vigor

UW-W: Balance in love and pleasure; love a matter of decisions rather than emotion; pleasure/love test balance; retribution in love

13. ᚻ Wisdom Collated/Life Changes (Path to Underworld)

Onn in:

OW-N: Wisdom emphasized through opportunity; life changes due to age/wisdom gathered

OW-E: Opportunity for abundance; bountiful wisdom

OW-S: Happiness from opportunity and wisdom applied to create life changes

OW-W: Positive changes from gathered wisdom lead to peace; inspiration generates life changes

MW-N: Challenge causes positive changes; friction in life changes overcome through gathered wisdom

MW-E: Wisdom harvested; prosperity from knowledge; opportunity for gains from education/learning

MW-S: Contentment from gathered knowledge and positive changes; harmony in life changes

MW-W: Increased knowledge emphasized resulting in opportunities/positive changes/new life

UW-N: Ending of harmony; transformation through gathered knowledge and wisdom emphasized; rapid changes for the better

UW-E: Growth of opportunity; increase in positive changes; youthful approach to life

UW-S: Energy to implement life changes; vitality of knowledge and wisdom; energetic changes

UW-W: Knowledge increases capacity for love/pleasure; wisdom in love; opportunity in love; positive changes in love/pleasure

14. ᚛ Insight/Foreknowledge/Enlivening (Path to Underworld)

Luis in:

OW-N: Insight in age; ability in foreknowledge enhanced

OW-E: Abundance of insight; power of healing; great activity

OW-S: Happiness in creativity; able to find own bliss; relief; using insight to bring happiness; joyfully active

OW-W: Healing; inspiration enhances creativity

MW-N: Challenge leads to increase in activity; argument clears the air; friction in creativity; insight leads to friction

MW-E: Prosperity from insight/healing; foreknowledge used wisely; successful creativity; fruitful activity

MW-S: Contentment in creativity; insight brings contentment; harmonious activity

MW-W: Learning healing; knowledge of healing; insightfulness; creative learning

UW-N: Transformation from insight; endings/new beginnings brought about through healing; new activities

UW-E: Youthful activities; growth of insight; creativity enhanced

UW-S: Energy for activities; vitality of insight; healing energy

UW-W: Healing love; insightfulness in love; creativity brings pleasure

15. ⚡ Developing Skills/Learning (Path to Underworld)

Gort in:

OW-N: Gains in due time; increasing wisdom

OW-E: Abundance by persistence; developing skills lead to favorable results; learning brings gains

OW-S: Joy of learning; happiness is attained by tenacity

OW-W: Peace comes through tenacity; inspired to learning;new skills discovered

MW-N: Challenge in persistence; friction leads to new skills developed; difficult studies

MW-E: Prosperity from new skills; gains from persistence

MW-S: Contentment found in new skills/learning; harmony comes with effort and persistence

MW-W: Learning emphasized; learning involves new skills; gains in knowledge through hard work/tenacity

UW-N: Hard work pays off; persistence transforms into tangible gains; transformation through learning

UW-E: Growth from learning; growth of skills; gains in youth through persistence

UW-S: Energy to gain goals through tenacity; vitality of learning; energy to develop skills

UW-W: Pleasure in a new skill/learning; persistence in love succeeds

16. ⊥ Truth/Endurance/Strength (Path to Underworld)

Duir in:

OW-N: Endurance of wisdom; longevity

OW-E: Abundance through strength/willpower

OW-S: Happiness found in truth/inner strength

OW-W: Inspiration of truth; willpower brings peace

MW-N: Able to endure challenges; overcome obstacles

MW-E: Endurance/willpower beings results; prosperity in truth; solid achievements

MW-S: Contentment from overcoming obstacles; harmony in truth; creating own contentment through willpower

MW-W: Learning truth; overcome obstacles to learning; strength in knowledge

UW-N: Positive force applied to create transformation; ending of obstacles; truth revealed

UW-E: Ability to overcome obstacles leads to growth; growth through willpower; youthful strength

UW-S: Vitality of truth; energy to overcome obstacles; energy enhances strength; vitality of willpower

UW-W: Use of determination to secure love; truth in love; love conquers all

17. † Rulership/Vigor/Discernment

Ailm in:

OW-N: Discretion in wisdom; vigor in age; secret wisdom

OW-E: Discrete use of bounty; vigorous abundance

OW-S: Discretion ensures happiness; happiness in rulership; vigor in bliss

OW-W: Secret inspiration; discretion in peace

MW-N: Challenge met with discrete rulership; vigorous response; secrecy breeds friction

MW-E: Prosperous rulership; gains from discretion/secrecy; vitality in prosperity

MW-S: Harmony from discretion; contentment in rulership

MW-W: Learning discretion; secret knowledge; aptitude for learning; leader in education

UW-N: Secrecy leads to transformation; new openness; transformation of rulership

UW-E: Growth of rulership; growth of discretion/secrecy; youthful vigor

UW-S: Vigor emphasized; energy for rulership

UW-W: Secret love; discretion in pleasure; vigorous love; dominance in love

18. ⊬ Introspection/Other Sight

Muin in:

OW-N: Introspection in age; introspective wisdom

OW-E: Bounty from other sight; introspection leads to abundance

OW-S: Happiness from looking inward

OW-W: Inspiration from introspection; peace through reflection

MW-N: Challenge in self-analysis; friction leads to introspection

MW-E: Rewards reaped from reflection/introspection

MW-S: Contentment found by introspection, harmony based upon reflection

MW-W: Learning through introspection/reflection; knowledge comes from within/from other sight

UW-N: Transformed by introspection/other sight

UW-E: Growth from looking inward

UW-S: Energy turned to introspection; reflective youth

UW-W: Introspective approach to love

19. ⊤ Beginnings/Energy

Beithe in:

OW-N: Beginnings of wisdom; energetic age

OW-E: Abundant energy; auspicious beginnings

OW-S: Happiness from new beginning; energy for bliss

OW-W: Beginnings of inspiration; unseen forces lead to inspiration and peace

MW-N: Challenge pushes for new beginning; energy from friction

MW-E: Beginning of period of prosperity; energy to bring matters to fruition

MW-S: Contentment from new beginnings; harmony with the unseen forces of growth

MW-W: Beginning of learning/knowledge; energy for learning; subtle growth of knowledge

UW-N: Ending leads to a new beginning; transformative energy; transformed by growth

UW-E: Growth emphasized; youthful energy; growth leads to new beginning

UW-S: Energy emphasized; vitality in new beginning; vitality of quiet growth

UW-W: Beginning of love/pleasure; unseen forces of growth that work in love; energy for love/pleasure

20. ⊥ Pleasure/Misfortune/Cleansing

Huath in:

OW-N: Pleasure in wisdom; comfortable old age; positive changes in age

OW-E: Enjoyment of abundance

OW-S: Cleansing brings happiness

OW-W: Inspirational cleansing; stimulating peace; positivity

MW-N: Challenge/friction may lead to misfortune or positive changes

MW-E: Harvest what is sown as either pleasure or misfortune; prosperity from positive changes/cleansing

MW-S: Harmony emphasized; contentment from cleansing

MW-W: Knowledge leads to positive changes; pleasure in learning

UW-N: Endings bring a positive change; transformation through cleansing

UW-E: Growth of pleasure; youthful pleasures; growth brings cleansing

UW-S: Energy for positive changes; vitality for pleasure

UW-W: Pleasure emphasized; enjoyment of love; care needed to avoid misfortune in love

21. | Cosmic Influence/Destiny/Fate

Blank in:

OW-N: Destiny/cosmic influence in *Age; Wisdom*

OW-E: Destiny/cosmic influence in *Abundance*

OW-S: Destiny/cosmic influence in *Happiness*
OW-W: Destiny/cosmic influence in *Light; Gentleness; Inspiration*
MW-N: Destiny/cosmic influence in *Conflict; Resistance; Challenge*
MW-E: Destiny/cosmic influence in *Prosperity; Harvest*
MW-S: Destiny/cosmic influence in *Harmony; Contentment*
MW-W: Destiny/cosmic influence in *Learning; Knowledge*
UW-N: Destiny/cosmic influence in *Endings; Transformation*
UW-E: Destiny/cosmic influence in *Growth*
UW-S: Destiny/cosmic influence in *Vitality; Energy*
UW-W: Destiny/cosmic influence in *Love*

Method of Throwing the Fews

The fews of the ogham may be drawn on pebbles, on sticks of wood, or tiles. You might want to use the matching type of wood for each few if you can find them all. Sometimes lumber stores or home repair/building supply stores will have a variety of woods from which you could gather chips for the fews. The symbols can also be carved into the wood. Fews can also be made from wood edging that can be bought at lumber/home supply stores. These often come with designs on one side, and you can then etch the few symbol on the other side.

Some people like to pull a specific number of fews from a bag and lay them out in a pattern reminiscent of tarot spreads, applying the ogham worlds to the spread. You could place one few in each realm and read them like that, but my preference is to hold the fews in my hands while I focus on a question, then lightly toss them up into the air over the casting cloth to let them land in a scattered fashion.

After tossing the fews over the cloth, look at where the fews have landed and how they landed. Some will be upside down, while others will be off the casting cloth. These you remove and set aside or return to the pouch. They do not play a role in the reading. Others may be sideways, and may be removed if they do not give easy access to their symbols—or they can be read as an underlying or peripheral influence. Fews that overlap each other show a strong connecting influence. Fews that overlap the realms show an influence that is either in both realms or in motion leading from one realm to another. The fews closest to the center have greater influence on the reading than those at the outer edges of the casting cloth.

Look over the casting cloth as though you are looking at a map, because, in a way, that is what the cloth becomes for you—a map that shows the route you will travel to answer your question. As with any divination, the throw shows how things are currently laid out. Once you can see that, you can then make adjustments to create changes, which again, is the purpose of magic and witchcraft.

Start with the few closest to the center of the cloth—the midhe. You always begin in Middleworld, because that is where you are. Determine how you will follow the fews before you attempt to start the reading. You will be moving clockwise in a spiral, starting from the centermost few. Once you have plotted out the path on which the fews will take you, you can begin the reading.

One easy way to remember when you are encountering a path few is to realize that there are five ways of drawing the ogham letters, and there are one to five branches on a tree (letter) with the exception of the one blank few (the mistletoe). So fives are Otherworld; fours are paths to Otherworld; threes are Middleworld; twos are paths to Underworld; and ones are Underworld. The paths move in both direction. When you begin the reading in Middleworld, and encounter a 2- or a 4-branched few, the reading moves to Underworld or to Otherworld and the few is read with the position in both Middleworld and the world to which it leads. So duir (oak) in MW-N, for example, would be read there, then also in UW-N, where it takes you. The reading continues in the world where the path took you until another path few is encountered. If it is a 4-branched few, you move through the midhe into the same quarter in Otherworld, and the reading continues there. If you then come to another 4-branched few, you are moved back into Middleworld.

Symbolically, you are moving back and forth through the central midhe of the worlds then reconnecting in the same realm in another world. Being in Underworld, as in our example, the reading continues with the fews having the UW interpretations. Suppose now you encounter a 4-branched few, such as eadha (aspen), in UW-S. You read the few interpretation for that placement, then you move into Otherworld and read the meaning for eadha in OW-S. Now the reading remains in Otherworld until you encounter another path few. Suppose you come to another 4-branched few, coll (hazel) in OW-W, for example. Since you are already in Otherworld, this path few takes you out of Otherworld and back to Middleworld. You read coll in OW-W and then again in MW-W, and continue in your spiral reading of the fews in Middleworld until you encounter another path few.

Assignment

1. List the 21 ogham fews by symbol and tree association. Check the listing in the chapter and see how well you remembered them.

2. List the 21 ogham trees by both Celtic and English names (example: duir-oak). Check your list against the listing in the chapter.

3. List the twenty-one ogham fews, and now look at the interpretations for the major arcanum of the tarot listed on text pages 122–124. Try matching each ogham few with a major arcana card from the tarot. What reason would you give for the match? Check the next page for one possible comparison. Is your list similar? Did you use the unnumbered card, THE FOOL?

Answers to Questions

1. and 2. Practice these exercises to become more familiar with the names and what the symbols look like. The sounds are usually quite soft—fearn is pronounced vern, eadha is eadth, and so forth.

3. Were you able to find a correlation between the images of the tarot and those of the ogham? There is no "right" listing. This is an exercise in working with universal archetypes. The shadings and nuances of the various decks emphasize the interpretation you as a reader might use. The ogham, too, will have differences in interpretation due to subtle variances in the reader's perspective. The more you work in different divination mediums, the more you come to define your own vision of the archetypes. These are the symbols that work for you and will transfer from one avenue of expression to another, but you should have a reason for your associations. See how your list compares to the following suggestions:

FOOL/the querent—the person embarking upon the quest of knowledge and understanding; the Wyrd (Blank) could also apply as Destiny

MAGICIAN/Iodho—controlling destiny matched with transformation

HIGH PRIESTESS/Coll—both relate to perception and wisdom, but Saille could be another match here for intuition

EMPRESS/Ur—gains and things coming to fruition

EMPEROR/Tinne—building and responsibilities matched with Ailm for rulership

HIGH PRIEST/Luis—organizing a spiritual path matched with insight and enlivening

LOVERS/Huath—this can be making choices matched with cleansing

CHARIOT/Eadha—dominance matched with overcoming obstacles

STRENGTH/Duir—two images of strength, power, and endurance

HERMIT/Gort—for the increase of wisdom

WHEEL/Wyrd—the turning of Fortune seen as Fate or Destiny

JUSTICE/Tinne—both represent balance

HANGED MAN/Fearn—meditation seen as leading to inner awareness and strength

DEATH/Ngetal—changes seen as inner development, transformation, but this could also be Onn for life changes

TEMPERANCE/Onn—harmony from use of common sense matched with the accumulated wisdom that leads to life changes

DEVIL/Ruis—seen as change/evolution or the natural course of things

TOWER/Straif—disruptive power that forces changes, a kind of coercion

STAR/Beithe—opportunities matched with new beginnings and energy

MOON/Saille—both show intuition and psychic power; flexibility

SUN/Muin—achievement matched with renewal and tenacity

JUDGEMENT/Quert—for the aspect of immortality and regeneration

WORLD/Nion—the ash as the World Tree; or Iodho for good conclusions

Class 6

Review; Stones & Crystals; Elixir Preparations; Inhabitation of Crystals and Stones; Obsidian Scrying

Review

Rules of Conduct

Here are the five rules of conduct to review once more. As you recite them to yourself, be mindful of what they mean to you and your relationship with The Power you seek to draw upon in your work. Think of how you apply these rules to your Craft and daily activities.

- Be careful what you do

- Be careful who you trust

- Do not use The Power to hurt another because what is sent comes back

- Never use The Power against someone else who has The Power

- To use The Power you must feel it in your heart and know it in your mind

Set Up the Altar

What kind of altar or working area are you in the mood to create? Do you feel that a ritualistic altar is what you want? Or perhaps something simple and cozy like a candle and incense? Look over the things that have meaning to you and see how you can incorporate them into your altar or your circle. If you like gardening, you may want to decorate your altar with clay pots, herbs, a bouquet of flowers, seed packets, and so forth. You could represent the Lady and the Lord with different flowers: a flower pot for her and seeds for him, or different garden tools. Use your imagination to creatively draw the Divine close to you.

Suppose your interests lie in music. Then think about the various items of music that could be part of your altar area or could mark the Quarters. Many people like to incorporate in their rituals instruments such as flutes, drums, and rattles, so you can bring these to your altar. Make it be inviting to you—a statement of your personality and individuality.

Cast the Learning Circle

Continuing with the gardening theme as an example, you might want to delineate your circle with string or twine used to stake up your tall plants. You could mark off the Quarters or surround yourself with flowers, garden tools, clay pots and saucers, seed packets, a scattering of flowers, herbs, or bulbs; with musical in-struments or tokens of these items: guitar picks, flute reeds, or tuning pipes.

You have read several different ways to cast the circle, so pick one of these methods for your circle, or create one for yourself. The format is the same, the items in brackets are optional

- Announce your intent to cast the circle
    (call upon light and the Elementals)

- Draw the circle
    (consecrate the circle with salt and water)
    (cense the circle)

- Call upon the Elementals at the Quarters
  (call upon the Lady and the Lord)

- Greet the Elementals, (Lady and Lord)
  (Honor the Lady and the Lord with the salted water
  and with the incense—see page 172 of the text)
  (pour a libation to the Lady and the Lord)

- Begin your circle activity

At the completion of your work, you may take some refreshment, perhaps referring to the tabbed section "Cakes and Wine" (text page 156). Before opening the circle, give your blessing to farewell the Lady and the Lord. Farewell the Elementals at each Quarter, bless the beings and powers of the visible and invisible, and announce that the circle is cleared. Open the circle, taking the light back into your athame, wand, or power hand. Announce

A learning circle outlined with living flowers and plants.

the ending of the ceremony and put away your magical tools. Empty the libation bowl into the earth or into the sink under running water.

Affinity of Stones and Crystals to Witchcraft

Elemental Earth

Stones and crystals are of the earth, and are easily utilized as representing the Elemental Earth. When creating your circle, you could use a stone to designate the north Quarter. But because of their versatility, you can use these for the other Elementals, based on the attributes of the stones and crystals. Thus, Earth might be a granite rock, Air a clear quartz crystal or calcite, Fire a red jasper, lava, or pumice, Water a river stone, or a blue stone such blue agate, aquamarine, turquoise, lapis lazuli, or even an azurite with mixture of blues and greens. You can use a series of stones and crystals to outline the circle, and have the Quarters indicated with special stones. Generally accepted qualities of various stones and crystals are listed in chapter 8 of *Green Witchcraft II*.

These are the bones of the earth, and contain the power to aid in your own grounding. When you are stressed out or scattered in your thoughts and emotions, hold a large stone in your hands (a 3–5 pound rock is about right). Envision the static energies gathering together and moving up from your feet, up your legs and into your abdomen, pushing further up past your stomach, while energy moves downward from your head and past your throat. The energy coming downward begins to pool around your shoulders and upper chest with the energy moving upward. Now, with the stone resting in your hand, see these turbulent energies cascade as twin waterfalls, down your arms, through your hands, and into the stone. Feel the stone pulse and grow warm with this energy.

Bless the energy within the stone:

I bless you, fire of life, that though you were excessive for me to hold, may the Mother Earth receive you that you may work for her well-being.

Lay the stone on the ground and cover it with dirt. This allows the energy to dissipate in the earth, to be utilized for healing or growth as the Earth sees fit. After three days, you can retrieve your stone. Wash it off (using a garden hose is fine) and put the stone in a container where you can then cover it with spring water. Let it soak for another three days for cleansing, remove from the water and let dry in the sun. Your grounding stone is ready to use again.

Stones have been the focus of imaging energy for thousands of years. The megaliths of the stone age still have a power that can be felt today. We stand in awe of the stone circles and towering rows of upright stones erected by our prehistoric ancestors. That sensation stirring within is the result of energy fields interacting with the cellular energy fields of our bodies. The power of these ancient sites has not gone away. The great earthworks in Midwestern America, built by the Native American Mississippian cultures, and the stone circle of the Sun and other such sites of the Anasazi in Four Corners (where the states of Colorado, New Mexico, Arizona, and Utah meet) and Mesa Verde are New World locations that generate the same sense of timelessness and connection through time with our ancestors. Performing magic ritual or working with crystals in such an atmosphere is charged with energy—caution is recommended.

Crystals often reside in what appear to be rough, round rocks, called geodes. Tap one with a hammer and it splits apart to reveal a hollow inner chamber lined with crystal points. A large, flat bed of amethyst is excellent for storing a crystal after use. The bottom of the amethyst bed is rock—grounding and earthy. The points of the purple crystal offer spiritual cleansing. Rinse off a crystal that has been used for a healing, for example, and let it drain resting overnight on the amethyst bed. The healing crystal is cleansed and ready to be used again, and the amethyst can be rinsed off and dried inverted on its points. Geodes hold all kinds of lovely secrets. Sometimes a rock will reveal an inner pocket of water. This is a real find! Here are the Elementals of the early Earth—millions of years old—with the water of life held within an air bubble inside the body of earth formed in the fires of transformation. Such a geode would be excellent on an altar. There is a tangible, living essence within that speaks to the Elementals and The Power.

Passage for Other Sight

Stones and crystals have an established history as excellent meditation tools. The popular crystal ball is the most widely known use of crystals for divination. Balls fashioned from natural rock crystal are very expensive. Less expensive are balls made of lead crystal, and even less expensive are those made of glass. Obsidian, malachite, and other polished stones are also used to make divination balls. When scrying, the type of object does not really matter. Natural crystal will not be a better tool if you are not able to divine by visions, whereas any tool will work for divination by vision. Crystal users will generally assign one task to each stone.

When you acquire any ball for divination, wash it in running water, then dry it off. Set it atop a pentacle on your altar while you heat up some mugwort tea. Use the Consecration of a tool ritual (pages 173–176 of the text) to prepare your crystal for use. Bathing the crystal in cool mugwort tea activates the crystal or polished stone for divination.

After the consecration, hold the object in your hands and look it over, rather like getting acquainted. You can peer at all the facets and find images and focal points while letting the stone or crystal get to know you. Your mind should be contemplating the desired use of this object as you explore.

For divination, seek out the center of the ball, but do not let yourself go out of focus. Some of my students have said their vision blurs and they just don't see anything, but the key to divination is not to go out of focus. It is a matter of relaxing and casually focusing on the center. If there is a flaw or bubble in the ball, this is a good place to direct your attention. If you find you are constantly shifting your sight to another part of the crystal, you are not ready to use this particular object for divination—you are still getting acquainted, as it were.

Crystal meditation and traveling occurs by the same method as with any other ball. The difference is that once you are able to perceive the crystal as coming to you and surrounding you (or you entering the crystal and being surrounded by it) you can then ask to see whatever it is you are interested in, or you may ask to travel. Natural crystals contain energy fields that will interact with your own, so it is important to properly cleanse and program the crystal prior to use. Once this is done, do not allow others to handle your crystal, lest they imprint it with their own energies.

When you travel within the ball, you can visit other worlds, dimensions, or locations. Sometimes it is easiest to "test" a ball by seeking images of a place or event you can later verify. If you need to close your eyes to visualize something, then you may find it hard to see images in balls, water, or mirrors. However, the ability to visualize without closing your eyes grows with practice, so do not believe it beyond you. It is rather like returning to the childhood awareness within you. Remember when you rode an invisible horse or traveled in a spaceship made out of a cardboard box? The child's ability to visualize and turn a table with a sheet over it into a house, a cottage in the enchanted woods, or a castle is the same kind of visualization exercise that will enable you to focus and "see" in a divination ball.

Stones can be a source of focus for the Earth Goddess and Earth God. Stones have been identified with deities throughout the world for thousands of years, into the paleolithic past. The idea of idols may have come from a desire to retain and transport to other places the energy felt at a natural rock place. A sense of Divine presence exists in rocks all over the world, from Ayers Rock in Australia to Crom Cruliach (also written as Cenn Cruaich) in Ireland. India has rocks identified with Shiva and with Shakti, and in Southwestern America, the Native Americans have their sacred rock mountain. Sacred rocks are recognized for the palpable energy emanating from them.

Some rocks are more symbolically used as fertility representations. Natural round stones with holes in the centers—yoni, or holey stones—are universally recognized as generating the goddess power of birth. Natural pillar stones are seen as phallic representations—lingam stones. Women seeking to bear children would (and still do!) walk naked through a holey stone, or sit naked atop a lingam stone. For those who scoff at the notion, there are babies born to refute the disbelief. The energies of these stones are primal, directing fertile emanations from the Earth into whatever is contacted.

Multiple Elemental Representation

When you look over the listing of stones and crystals in *Green Witchcraft II*, you can see from their applications that some types align well with the Elemental Earth, Air, Fire, and Water. You can use these stones at the Quarters of your ritual circles, to represent the Elemental power, or you can use the stones in spellwork to designate the energy of a particular Elemental. On the following pages is a list of stones and crystals by Elemental aspect (some stones and crystals have multiple applications, depending on the energy utilized):

EARTH	AIR
agate (all but blue-lace)	amethyst
apache tear	aquamarine
apatite	azurite
aventurine	beryl
boji stone	blue lace agate
calcite (orange)	carnelian
carnelian	chalcopyrite (peacock stone)
diamond	chrysocolla
fluorite	chrysoprase
granite	citrine
iron pyrite	diamond
jade	fluorite
jasper (brown, green)	hematite
jet	kyanite
malachite	lazurite
morion crystal (nearly black)	moldivite
onyx (all colors but black)	opal
petrified wood	pearl
rutilated quartz	snow quartz
rhodinite	sapphire
ruby	silver
staurolite	sodalite
sugilite	topaz (blue)
tiger eye	topaz (yellow)
tourmaline (black, green)	tourmaline (blue)
unikite	turquoise (blue)
	vivianite

FIRE	WATER
amber	alexandrite
beryl	aqua-aura
bloodstone	auricalcite
calcite (gold)	beryl
carnelian	calcite (green, orange)
citrine	chalcedony
coal	diamond
diamond	dioptase
flint	emerald
geodes	jacinth
gold	jade
jasper (red)	jet
lorimar	kunzite
obsidian	lapis-lazuli
peridot	magnetite
pumice	moonstone
quartz (smokey)	obsidian
rhodochrasite	onyx (black)
rhodinite	opal
sunstone	peridot
	quartz (rose)
	river rock
	rock crystal
	sardonyx
	topaz (blue)
	tourmaline (pink, watermelon)
	turquoise (green)
	zircon

Class 6

Using Stones and Crystals

Stones in Craft Workings

The type of stone or crystal used in magic or ritual is determined by the coloration, size, shape, and ages-old, recognized characteristics. My mother always told me that opals should only be used by people born in October, and I have heard others say much the same thing—only use opals if they are your birthstone. Today you can find opals listed in magic and Craft books for use for psychic power, astral travel, relaxation, and meditation. While these are all attributes and uses for opal, unless it is your birth sign I would recommend using some other stone. Amethyst, azurite, garnet, hematite (especially good for astral travel), moldavite, pearl (also well-suited for astral projection), and staurolite (brown-colored natural "Fairie Cross") all may be utilized for the same effects as opal. My mother cautioned that opals bring bad luck to anyone else, and I accept her tradition and take her word for it, but as in all matters of the Craft, you must determine whether or not this applies to you.

Chapter 8 of *Green Witchcraft II* also contains a ritual for redirecting the dedication of a crystal should the need arise. These minerals can be activated in the manner shown in that chapter, or by the method described in the next section (pp. 121–124). Some stones or crystals are more attuned to healing, while others enhance or augment the energy raised for magical workings. Witch jewelry is therefore very highly charged and very personal; only the owner should handle these items. This kind of jewelry—especially a combination of amber and jet—is consistently used in ritual and spell work, and the energy within the stones combines with the wearer to aid in raising, focusing, and setting energies.

Occasionally you may want to add stones directly into your magical work. Stones or crystals can be included inside a dream pillow to attract a desired result, to ward harm, or to soothe as the case may be. They can be laid out in an area for warding, protection, or cleansing; sewn into charms; programmed and carried in a small pouch around the neck; or added to a spell mixture.

One of the most powerful stones to add to a spell is jet. This stone can be called upon to bind into the spell the energy that is raised. A candle spell with symbols enscribed, anointed with oil, and burned with herbs dropped into it as the spell is chanted or stated is enhanced by the final addition of jet to bind the raised energy to the spell. After the spell is completed and the candle has burned for an hour (or however long your spell requires), snuff out the candle and let it cool. Before disposing of the candle, remove the jet, cleanse, and store it away from light. I keep my jets in a special pouch and when I need to use one, I cleanse it and dedicate it for the new use. The cleansing ritual is found on pp. 168–172 of the second text.

Cleansing Crystals Before Use

Quartz crystals are used in technology for radios and lasers, so it is not unreasonable to see their potential for use in psychic ways for amplifying your energy or activating the energy impulses that are normally found in body cells and brain activity. While the use of crystals is already accepted in scientific ways, the psychic level of interaction is not as readily verified, but to the witch, psychic phenomenon is a matter of course. It is not odd or unusual to communicate with spirits or converse with the Elementals or the Lady and the Lord—it is normal and natural.

Crystals are used every day in modern technology as potent generators, transformers, or transferers of energy. The understanding of crystals as able to interact with the individual on a personal level is another matter, more likely to involve documented cases only with minimal scientific explanation. Yet the psychic use of crystals has a longer tradition in human history than the scientific. The difference is that with natural crystal, the witch feels there is a living entity within. You can talk to a crystal and expect it to understand.

When you acquire a natural crystal, you need to cleanse it of extraneous energy patterns that it may have picked up from being mined and handled—particularly if touched by numerous people in a store setting. The crystal is affected by the energies of the people handling it, and the energy patterns become confused or diffused, so that until it is cleansed, the crystal will not function well. If you use such a crystal, you may feel nervous, agitated, fuzzy-headed, and otherwise not quite yourself. Indeed, if you are sensitive, you may even pick up on other people's energies and mistake these as your own. Energy-depletors could become attached to you if they handle a crystal that you later purchase.

I have heard people talk about "psychic vampires"—people who leech your energy stores and leave you feeling drained and lethargic after they leave your presence. These people actually have a naturally low-energy profile, and when they come into your presence, the energy levels between the two of you will come into balance. The low-energy person pulls off some of your energy until you are both equalized. The usual result is not that the other person is suddenly invigorated, but that you are less energized. The other person has more energy, but not at your original level, so that overall, instead of one person feeling down, you will both feel down, but in different degrees. People who are unable to retain energy may have gaps in their energy fields through which energy slips away. This is when psychic healers look at auras for weak areas to treat and repair with the transformative and focusing energies of natural crystals. If an energy-depletor has handled your crystal, you need to break any connection to that person by cleansing the crystal and attuning it to your own personal energies.

Another possibility with natural crystals is that you can inadvertently open a channel to another person through a crystal you have both handled. You might not even know the person, yet you will pick up sensations from them and transfer your own. When psychics handle an object to learn about a person—as is seen with aiding in police investigations—the sensitive person is feeling the energy residues left on the object. The same happens with natural crystals, and so they need to be cleansed.

The cleansing of a natural crystal is a little different from the method used with manufactured lead crystal, yet all stones and manufactured tools can be cleansed in this same way. I rinse out a cauldron with blessed water (saved from a Sabbat or Esbat), then wash the cauldron in cool, running water (from the tap is fine). I dry it, and set it on top of a wooden pentacle on my altar. Next I pour in some sea salt to coat the bottom of the cauldron, then place the crystal on top of the salt. More salt is poured over the crystal until it is buried. Using this method of cleansing, I have practically heard crystals give an audible sigh of relief— "Ahhh." The covering of the crystal with the salt gives it a chance to clear, and the life essence within is happy to get a rest from the cacophony of energy impulses.

Leave the crystal covered from two to seven days. Two is for balance, seven for completion. It really depends on how eager you are to use the crystal. For immediate use, you can employ the Consecration of a Tool ritual as noted previously, then use visualization to clear a crystal and attune it to yourself. You can program it by holding it at your psychic point (called the third eye), the center of your forehead, just above your eyes. Hold the crystal in your hand and see it as cleared, then see your own white aura expand outward from the center of your body, driving away any darkness. The darkness that your aura touches is transformed and you use it to cleanse the crystal in your hand. The visual image is rather like the white rapids of an advancing floodwater, with the churning portion being the transformation point of contact between light and dark energies, then the cleansing energy moving on so the cascade is in progressing motion away from you.

Witches who acquire a crystal and cleanse it should themselves also be cleansed. This is done by bathing in water enhanced with herbs and sea salt, swimming in the ocean, or using a sponge bath with water mixed with sea salt. If you cannot get sea salt (most grocery stores carry this) you can substitute rock salt (also found in grocery stores, generally labeled as good for making homemade ice cream). You can also use Dead Sea salt, which is often scented with the cleansing herb, lavender, and is usually found in the bath soaps and powders section of pharmacies. Salt baths are very refreshing and invigorating, and also good for the skin.

Some writers suggest more or less complicated rituals or routines for cleansing a crystal, but this is what I use. Another method is to soak the crystal in warm water mixed with sea salt, letting it sit for two to three days, then pouring out the used water and rinsing off the crystal in clear running water. It is a matter of preference, but I feel that salted water separates, so that the cleansing agent of the salt settles at the bottom of the container.

After cleansing by whichever method, rinse the crystal in cool running water and it is ready to be attuned to your needs. The sea salt contains the residue of chaotic energies, but you do not need to toss out the salt. Instead, once you have removed the stones and crystals, pour the salt into another container. Do this outdoors where the wind can pass through the pouring salt, releasing the energies into the care of the wind. In witchcraft, the wind is an aspect of the powerful Elemental Air, capable of dissipating the energies. If there is no breeze, call upon Elemental Air to send the West Wind or the North Wind to you (for transitions). Now the salt should be placed into a dark container with a tight lid, until the next time you need it.

Crystals in Craft Workings

Review the listing of crystals (pp. 117–118) to determine which kind you need for your work. Some crystals and stones are recognized as being inclined toward certain properties. You can determine which type of stone or crystal you need by the natural proclivity of the item. When you find one you can relate to, cleanse and program it so that its natural function can aid you.

Crystals can be clear, cloudy, or a combination of those characteristics. You will want to use them according to their predominant attributes. Clear quartz crystals will activate your energy levels and help with clarity of thought, assisting in energizing and focusing. Cloudy crystals are good for relief from stress and tension—rather like crystalline cotton balls saturated in a cooling astringent such as witch hazel. Envision the crystal as wiping away stress with cooling moisture that leaves the psyche feeling cleansed and restored. Even a mixture of clear and cloudy could be programmed for balance.

To work with crystals, you need to address the entity within. If you feel drawn to a crystal, it is probably reaching out to you. If you are not attracted to a crystal, it would be better left for someone else. You can activate the crystal energy by projecting into it your compassion or love for it and your desire to work with it. You need to actually feel this way to successfully bond with the crystal. The crystal will receive this and return the same to you, which you will feel as a warm glow.

Some crystal users speak of the crystal as a tool rather like a computer waiting to be programmed. Witches, however, see minerals as life forms that are simply a little different from animal or vegetable life forms. You may work successfully with crystals with either viewpoint. Some people feel that a metal pot confuses the energy and recommend other containers for cleansing, while others never address the matter. Since I make a bed of salt in my cauldron, place the crystal on top of it, then add more salt to cover the crystal, the crystal is not actually touched by metal.

I have observed that Green Witchcraft is pantheistic and animistic—crystal connection is one example of that. Everything has something of the Divine within, and when you touch that essence, you make a connection with it that may last a lifetime or only a few moments. Saying hello to a boulder as you walk by is a fleeting connection that is nevertheless rewarding. For long-term relationships, you need to let the crystal know you care about it, and actually want its companionship.

You need to let the crystal know what response you seek from it, be it to help with healing, spiritual growth, divination, memory enhancement, protection, meditation, or astral travel. Like stones, crystals may be used to empower your magical workings and spell crafting materials, and to clarify your thoughts—making your ideas crystal clear. For aid in sleeping, use a cloudy crystal for release of stress and drawing of peace. For alertness, use a clear crystal. For intuitive skills, use a cloudy crystal. For active energy flow, use a clear crystal.

Programming a crystal to a particular purpose may be done by holding it in your power hand, connecting with the crystal by letting it feel your affection for it, then projecting an image that relates to what you want it to help with, while you think of the words that match the image. For example, for sleep aid, you could see yourself comfortably in bed, sound asleep. For memory enhancement, see a list, a journal, or a diary in which you record events. For dream recall, see a dream journal (many witches do write down dreams they find significant). Once your crystal is programmed, it only needs to be reminded of the image to help in that task. You can also program your crystal to cleanse other items or areas of negative energies by projecting the image of bright white light.

Although shopping with company is fun, if both of you are witches or attuned to the energy emanations of objects, a crystal could get confused. My daughter and I have often bought crystals together, only to discover once we got them into our separate magic areas that we had gotten the other's crystal. When that happens, the best thing to do is simply acknowledge the reality and give the crystal to the person it has reached out to. We are often drawn to the same crystal, but once alone with it, we can recognize who it was for. Keeping a crystal that you are not attuned with can cause headaches, tension, nervousness, and upset the digestive tract. Another source of discomfort for you may be that the crystal (after use) needs to be cleansed and drained on an amethyst bed as described earlier.

As with all tools of witchcraft, you should not let others handle your crystals. If someone does, cleansing is in order. For a quick purification, immerse the crystal for half an hour in a container of warm water mixed with sea salt and vinegar. Remove, rinse under cool running water, and let it drain on the amethyst bed or simply dry and store as usual. Toss out the soaking water since it will contain the purged energies.

Your stones and crystals can be used in spellwork. They can be infused with the magical intent, consecrated and dropped into candle magics, wrapped into a sachet, added to a dream pillow, or placed with the spell materials when buried. If used in candle magics, the stone may be used repeatedly simply by removing it from the wax when you are finished, washing it, and cleansing it again with the power of the Elementals. Store it in a dark cloth or away from light so it can regather its energies.

Place your stones in the light of the Full Moon or other cosmic entity for energizing. Dark Moon energizing is good for obsidian and other dark power stones. Eclipses help to energize stones for passage between the worlds.

Healing with Crystals

There are a lot of books available today for healing and otherwise working with crystals, but the basic thread is that you are attempting to heal and bring balance into someone's life. The cloudy and clear crystals act as an expression of the duality that goes directly back to the Divine as Lady and Lord in terms of nurturing and active energies. The two are used together to balance a person's aura when the person lies face-up, with the clear crystal pointed at the top of the head and the cloudy crystal pointed at the feet.

Place a smaller clear crystal in the right hand, pointing down, and a smaller cloudy crystal in the left hand, pointing up. This gives the energy field a circular movement.

Using a crystal designated for healing, move this over the body, in a slow circular motion, down the right side and up the left. The crystal will pause over areas needing healing, and you will feel

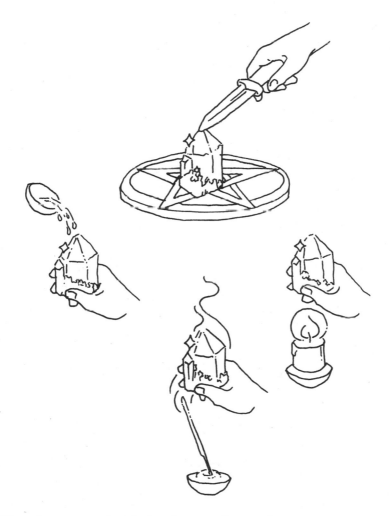

Charging a crystal with the elementals, Earth, Fire, Water, and Air.

additional heat from the crystal. When the crystal seems unwilling to move, and you feel heat or a prickling sensation from the crystal, project into it an image of light and compassion. This will radiate through the crystal and into the aura of the person being treated. Once your crystal feels balance is restored, you will sense it is ready to move on. When this is finished, have the person turn over to lie face down, and repeat for the back. After both sides of the person have been treated, have the person rest face-up for a few minutes with the crystals in place while you cleanse the one you have used for auric healing. Then take the other crystals and cleanse them while you and the person you worked on discuss the points where there were weaknesses or stress.

When used in healing, crystals can be selected also for their color. Look at the color listing in the text pages 63-64. The attributes of colors can be used in healing the lack of that attribute in a person's energy field. Feeling weak? Choose a red-tinged crystal for strength. Feeling indecisive? Choose an indigo crystal. Review the list and see it in terms of healing whatever a person may feel is lacking. Some examples of colored crystals are amethyst, citrine, emerald, flourite, moonstone, morion, peridot, rhodinite, rose quartz, smokey quartz, topaz, and tourmaline.

Crystals come in a range of colors to fit the energies desired which also draw you.

Bodily and Elemental Energy Points

Bodily Energy Points

There are a number of energy points of the body, and these are affected in different ways. In Green Witchcraft, *bodily energy points* exist along the body at the base of the spine, the abdomen, the stomach, the heart, the throat, above the area between the eyes, and at the top of the head. This does not quite match with the system of "chakras," although it is very close. From my mother's perspective, the energy points related to the very grounded manner of how the body functions throughout life.

Besides the sexual organs at the base energy point, there are openings into your interior body that require protection for your health. You can absorb negative energies, parasites, fungus, harmful bacteria, and so forth into yourself through these openings. Taking care of your body's vulnerable places was always part of understanding Nature. My mother's family has for several generations lived in Brazil where the people use a word that literally translates to "mushrooms" to describe an intestinal fungus people can acquire by swimming in the river waters. Unless a water supply is very clean, there is always the possibility of absorbing unwanted microbes into your body while swimming, especially if there is any kind of sewage or other pollution in the water. In the United States, E. coli bacteria has been known to spread from one infected person to other people swimming together in water parks and pools.

Sitting directly in the dirt or on the ground was discouraged, just as was walking barefoot (and in the southern states of America, this is indeed a way to get hookworms). It was okay to sit on the ground on a blanket or other covering, or to sit sideways on the ground, but never directly on the ground. For spell work, the area is always swept clean with the magically energized besom. Then the witch may work barefoot in a cleansed, protective environment, but my mother insisted on some kind of footwear if we were not indoors.

In witchcraft, there is a general tradition that touching the ground drains out energy. You touch your palms to the ground to drain out excess energy after spellwork; you are cautioned in some groups to not let your tools or magical herbs touch the ground lest they lose their powers. Yet in my family, it was not a problem for plants to touch the earth they grew up in, and tools could be quickly reinfused with energy by calling upon the Elementals while waving the tool through the air and focusing on the intent for the tool's use. However, draining your personal energy into the ground was avoided to keep from having to rebuild from that loss. Draining your energy reserves can lead to illness and leave you susceptible to negative energy fields. So the base energy point one is where the interior of the body makes contact with the outer world, and it needs proper health maintenance for the benefit of the body.

The second energy point is the intestinal area. The ancient Egyptians related emotions to the liver rather than the heart, and my mother included with the liver the action of the intestines. Today, psychology understands the "fight-or-flight" reaction of intense emotion, and this reaction may coincide with a sudden elimination of bodily waste. Watch a bird take flight in alarm, and you will see that the first thing it does is eliminate waste. The rude expression for this kind of fright is based on an uncontrollable natural reaction. But love, anxiety, worry, or anger can also send the intestines into turmoil and rapid elimination, so I feel that the Green Craft impression of the abdomen as an energy point has a foundation in ancient tradition.

The third energy point is around the stomach. This is where the foods eaten can work for you or against you. Here is the watershed of your energy-consumption for processing and distribution throughout your body. When you are sick, the stomach has difficulty processing food and you may experience appetite loss; when you eat inappropriate or unhealthy foods, your stomach is upset; when you are nervous, your stomach produces acid; and when you are excited, your stomach may disgorge its contents to allow energy to flow to other areas.

The fourth energy point is the heart. Here is the source of blood flow through the body, and when there is great stress, this muscle may react by increasing or decreasing the heartbeat. Some people in a time of stress feel their heart slow, the blood drains from their face, and they experience a sinking sensation. Others feel their heart beating rapidly, a rush of heat to their face, and a sensation of extreme agitation so severe that their body shakes. Reacting to events or emotions may cause the heart to pound violently, or to flutter. Whatever the action, there is no doubt that the heart is a vitally important organ, moving the blood rapidly through the body in times of need, and when soothed returning to its proper function.

The fifth energy point is the throat. When excited, the throat may constrict and make breathing difficult. Some people find they choke, cannot swallow food or drink, or lose their power of speech when animated or excited. This comes from an improper energy flow. When emotions lodge in the throat, energy flow is being blocked. You need to refocus on the flow of that excessive energy to visualize it passing through the arms and hands to the ground, or down the sides, into the legs, and through the feet to the ground. You do not want to run it through the body or the other energy points, or you will create negative reactions all along the route. Using the hands as exits usually works best, but be sure you can ground the energy by expelling it into something else. Here is when a grounding stone can be useful.

The sixth energy point is between and slightly above the eyes. When a person is anxious or disturbed about something, this point may become irritated, sore, or achy. People will rub this area with their hands in an instinctive reaction that produces temporary soothing. Clearing excess or agitated energy from this area can be done with the hands. Use both hands together at the center between the eyes, and wipe the hands across the forehead to either side, then shake the hands downward. Envision the tension, the irritating energy as drops of water, wiping them from the eyes and forehead, then shaking the drops off the hands so the energy falls to the ground where it is absorbed.

The seventh energy point is at the top of the head, and anyone who has experienced a headache at this point knows how powerful this site is. Here is where the body's heat radiates outward, which is why you need to keep your head covered in cold weather—your body heat will rise out. It is also where your body makes contact with the external energies that interact with the energies of the brain.

The brain is like a vast battery, the cells charging and discharging, directing activity throughout the physical body while reacting and acting in mental impulses of energy. Much of the energy generated by other people is drawn into the top of the head, so when you are confronted by people who are soothing and responsive, your head feels fine. When people are throwing negative energies at you, your head begins to throb from the overload. The brain is working hard now to equalize the energy, and this can result in energy being shifted down the body, into the other energy points, into the muscles, and into the organs.

A little preventative action can alleviate the problem. The technique of shielding is typical in witchcraft. You envision yourself in a protective bubble of your own creation—perhaps it is mirrored on the outside—and when the negative energy is thrown at you, you flip on your "shields" and see the energy bounce off, or reflect back to the sender.

Another protection is to wear a clear crystal that is programmed to repel unwanted negative energies. This can be part of a hair ornament, an earring, or it can be tucked inside a hat or hair band. Place it so the point is down, and when the energy attack occurs, visualize the flow diverted into the crystal, passed down your arm, out the palm of your hand, and into the ground. If you feel a bit annoyed, you can discreetly direct the palm of your hand at the person and savor the moment of the person's own energy hitting them back! I do not recommend this unless you plan to depart the presence of this person at once, because once the energy is sent back, the person will become even more charged. This will also give the person a very upset physical reaction. "Returning to sender" is a dark-sided magic method of handling negative energies that only an experienced witch should use and only when there is no suitable alternative, as when a negative attack occurs while you are on your own property.

Elemental Energy Points

Besides these bodily energy points, the Green Craft also recognizes the *Elemental energy points*—the palms of the hands and the soles of the feet. These are the sites where energy passes into and out of the body. Like the top of your head, body heat exits from these areas more than anywhere else, which is why in cold weather you need to wear warm socks and gloves or mittens. The left foot is Earth, and the right foot is Air, the right hand is Fire, and the left hand is Water. When you do magic, the motion of the hands draws in, focuses, and directs the Elemental powers, while the placement or motion of the feet grounds or raises energy. It is through these energy points that you can drain out excess or negative energies.

When you are seeking active results in your magical practice, the right hand is the influential one. You use this hand to draw in the power of Elemental Fire to energize and ignite your magic to accomplish your goals. The left hand is the one used to soothe, to draw upon the intuitive, perceptive, and flowing power of Elemental Water. This hand blesses and protects, while also urging matters to completion.

The left foot, when placed upon the ground, draws up into the witch the strength and power of Elemental Earth. By visualizing this energy coming up into yourself as you work your magics, you add that "groundedness" to your spell or charm that brings the magic into a physical manifestation. The right foot, raised in dance around the circle, gathers into the witch the power of Elemental Air. The motion of raising the right foot at an angle and then stepping it back down generates a palpable in-gathering sensation of spiritual, mental, and psychic energies. The left foot then transfers these nebulous or amorphous aspects of Elemental Air into solid, physical manifestation.

It is because these areas of the extremities of the body have such great ability to make direct contact with the Elemental energies that many witches prefer to perform their magics barefoot. The practice of working *skyclad*, or in the nude, takes this concept a step further so that the entire body of the witch is left open to channel, focus, and direct the powers being invoked.

Other Uses for Stones and Crystals

Elixir Preparations

Gem and stone elixirs are waters charged with the energies of the materials soaked in them. You can use elixirs in spell work, to asperge tools, or as a drink to heighten a particular energy within you. Gem/stone elixirs are included in chapter 8 of *Green Witchcraft II*, designated by an asterisk, with their general uses described in parenthesis. To make an elixir, soak a charged gem/stone in a cup of spring water for an hour during a Full Moon or Dark Moon, depending on the purpose of the elixir—Full for gaining, completion, or growing projects; Dark for banishing, ending, or clearing out projects. Then consecrate and store the elixir away from light. Drink as needed. You may want to add a drop of whiskey or brandy to "hold" the energies.

Elixirs can also be used as a wash on tools or spellworking objects to energize them with the attributes of the stone or crystal used in the elixir. They can be used to cleanse or prepare a candle prior to dressing it with an oil for a ritual.

Most spellwork and magical workings only require an hour at most for the desired effect. When you are done with your magics, remember to ground yourself by touching the floor or earth with the palms of your hands. Let that excess energy flow out so you are not jittery, have something to eat, and resume a normal routine.

Generator Crystals

To imbue a crystal with energies, you may want to keep one large crystal as a *generator*. This one is consecrated at the Full Moon, with fresh water from a running stream if at all possible, or with spring water. It is refreshed with the Full Moon and allowed to sit in the moonlight for a few hours—window sills are fine for this—then put away. When you want to realign a stone or crystal you have used in a spell, you can charge it by placing the generator crystal on it, and placing both on a pentacle on your altar. An hour is really all you need for this.

A generator crystal is usually the largest one you have. When the other crystals are not in use, they can be arranged around the generator for re-charging. When programming a generator, you may want to envision a bright beam of light coming from it to energize the other crystals. For the most part, visual imagery is the best method for communication with crystals, which is already a part of how we talk. When we say words, we have images for those words. When talking to your crystal for a focus of energy, remember to visualize the completed desire as you speak.

Communication with Your Crystal

You can talk to a crystal and expect it to understand because of the interconnection of all things through the Goddess and the God. In the Green path there is a union with other entities for working together. Since the witch is part of the life form of the Earth, one with the Elementals, who are kith and kin, and part of the Lady and the Lord as they are part of the witch, uniting with his or her crystal creates a close working relationship. The crystal becomes so attuned to the witch that it feels protective and bonded. The advantage here is that the crystal will actively seek to defend and protect the witch, and actively repel attempts by others to influence it. The crystal does the work it knows you want it to do—out of love. It will also recognize and more easily shed "non-you" energies. The crystal knows the sensation of "you" and reaches out to you when it senses your need.

To join with your crystal, hold it in your left hand at your heart energy point as you sit comfortably for meditation. Place your right hand under the left and project yourself into the crystal, thinking of it as a crystal tower (as in the tarot) or a house. When you see the crystal all around you, examine it carefully. Look at the walls, ceiling, floor; experience the textures within the crystal; sense the atmosphere for temperature, flavor, and scent; and listen to the sounds within the crystal. Feel the pulse of energy and move into the vibration so that your body has the same pulse and you can then flow into the walls of the crystal. With your energies and those of the crystal combined, you are united and bonded. To leave, simply regather yourself at the center of the crystal and move back into your own body. Rest a moment, and return to normal awareness through the breathing exercise previously covered in meditation. Ground the excess energy, have a snack, and perform some routine chore. After this, the crystal will activate simply by being held in your hand until its pulse matches yours.

Your crystal may also be *inhabited*. When you call upon a companion from Otherworld, or a spiritual presence, a crystal makes an excellent residence. Often you find by looking into a crystal that there is someone looking back at you. When you see visions within, landscapes and movement, this is a passage-crystal, a gateway to Otherworld. Not all crystals are like this, of course. If you have successfully called upon a companion (see the "Companion Quest" in *Green Witchcraft II*), you should look for a suitable crystal for this entity to inhabit from time to time. The crystal becomes a kind of talisman to carry with you, so you can feel the closeness of your companion at all times and can call upon the entity whenever you have need.

Basically, there are several options when working with crystals:

- The crystal can be used as a programmable energy source
- It can be seen as an entity that is part of the living Earth
- It can be the habitation of an energy entity
- It can be a portal to Otherworld
- It can become inhabited by a specific entity called upon in a ritual
- It can be temporarily occupied by energies or spirits for specific purposes

Not everyone will see things in a crystal or stone. The sense of a presence is something that is experienced individually. Your very action of inspecting a crystal or stone may act to draw an entity into it. When you do feel or see a presence within, look at the entity and examine the sensations reaching you. Are these sensations comforting? Friendly? Suspicious? Disinterested? Do you feel an attraction for the crystal that is reciprocated? If so, then it is meant for you. If not, the stone is probably meant for someone else.

Obsidian Scrying

Obsidian is the black, glass-like, and razor-sharp-edged stone formed by volcanic eruption. There is a lot of it in the area of Bend, Oregon, but it can also be found in the Pacific Northwest and the American Southwest. You can purchase smoothed and polished obsidian in mineral shops, rock shops, hobby shops, and New Age or occult supplies stores. Because of its hard, volcanic glass quality, obsidian can easily be used as a black mirror for meditation, vision seeking, and magical practice.

Like crystals, obsidian can also be used for companion questing and spirit habitation. It is a natural tool for travel to the Underworld and communing with the Lady and the Lord in their dark aspects of Crone and Lord of Shadows. In *Green Witchcraft II* there are several examples of how to use a black mirror for meditation, scrying, visions, and dark power magics. These same techniques can be applied to obsidian.

The one advantage that obsidian has over a black mirror is the living connection with the earth. Like all stones, crystals, and rocks, this volcanic glass has within it the essence and life-force of the earth. It is a living connection between the Underworld of the molten core of the planet and the Middleworld crust upon which we live. As such, obsidian can transfer immense energy from the inner stores of the earth to the practitioner.

When you look at a piece of obsidian, see if it is inhabited. Hold it in your hand and see if it changes. Does the rim warm and lighten? Do you detect movement within? Is there someone looking out at you? Do not be surprised or shocked if you see eyes gazing at you. Instead, focus on the sensation you feel. If the entity is friendly and offering companionship, and that is what you want, then the stone is for you. Otherwise, leave it alone.

Cleansing an obsidian piece is the same as with any crystal. When you dedicate it, you may prefer to use the Dark Moon phase and tailor its use to dark power aspects such as Underworld travels and spirit communication. I recommend washing the stone in cooled mugwort tea to attune the energies for magical focus, particularly for divination or Underworld scrying. Various types of divination lend themselves to obsidian, including viewing past lives and speaking with ancestors. It can be a very moving experience to call upon a vision of your ancestors. For a woman, seeing the faces of the ancestral matrons, the women through whose lineage your heritage can be truly traced, can result in a profound sense of grounding and connection.

Obsidian can be used in meditations to banish grief, to encourage spiritual healing, and to commune with Otherworld and Underworld. It is good for scrying, for Dark Aspect meditations, and for soothing help when going through traumatic changes. There is a soft, dark warmth to obsidian that makes it feel like a wooly blanket you can wrap around your psychic self for protection and comfort.

Assignment

1. Find a suitable grounding stone and consecrate it for your use (see pages 112–113 of this chapter).

2. Look for crystals or stones that help you to focus on the Elementals. These may be set on your altar or at the Quarters of your circle.

3. What are the bodily energy points?

4. What are the Elemental energy points?

5. What characterizes male and female crystals and what are their properties?

Answers to Questions

1. and 2. These are projects you may find helpful in your practice of the Craft.

3 In Green Witchcraft, *bodily energy points* exist along the body at the base of the spine, the abdomen, the stomach, the heart, the throat, slightly above and between the eyes, and at the top of the head.

4. The *Elemental energy points* are the palms of the hands and the soles of the feet. The left foot is Earth, and the right foot is Air, the right hand is Fire, and the left hand is Water.

5. The male crystal is clear and used to activate energies and aid and focusing. The female crystal is cloudy and used to soothe energies. It is good for relief from stress and tension, and can be used to cleanse and restore equilibrium to a person's energy field.

Class 7

Review; Consecration of a Statue;
Divine Couples; Holy Days &
Creating Your Own Calendar
of Observances;
Palmistry; Assignment

Review

The Rules of Conduct

Can you remember the Rules of Conduct? By now you should
have it down pretty well. Can you say them out of order? Do you
have your own words for some of the Rules? The meaning is
what is important, and much about the Rules can be applied to
daily life rather than only to magical practice. You need to be
careful about who you trust with your secrets and innermost
thoughts. You need to act with care so that you do not close off
relationships and opportunities for the future. You need to feel
confident about what you are doing for the best results. You need
to understand that negative energy draws negative energy, so of
course you want to take care in what you are generating. And
lastly, you need to look upon other witches as your cultural kin,

with whom you share a magical heritage, not as rivals. The idea of "witch wars" is contrary to the Rede and to Wiccan Initiation/ Dedications ceremonies.

Set Up the Altar

Another type of altar is the stang or the staff. This can be leaned upright against a table or chair, set into a stand, stuck into the ground, supported with stones, or even held upright by placing the end into an urn or vase. Stangs vary in size, and are usually two to three pronged, whereas staffs are single. The stang may be decorated with inscriptions in runic script or some other alphabet, painted, entwined with vines, or left plain.

A wreath made with herbs or plants appropriate for a ritual (evergreens for Yule, spring flowers for Ostara, and so forth) may also be hung on the stang, then returned to Nature afterward, or you could hang ribbons of different colors for the seasons from the stang. At the base, you can place a small table or some other flat surface where you can set incense and a candle to burn. Place there also a cup containing fruit juice or wine.

The stang or staff is set at the center of your learning area so you can sit at the base of it (or place it next to your chair as you read and work). Light the candle and the incense and you are ready to cast the circle. See text pages 57–59 and pages 63–64 for suggestions for selecting the incense and color of the candle best for you. What do you want the incense and candle color to represent? Spiritual knowledge? Achievement? Psychic awareness? Developing skills in witchcraft? For the latter, for instance, you can match amber incense with amber or jet candles.

Cast a Learning Circle

For this casting of the circle, all you are doing is calling upon positive energies to aid you in your study. The simplest circle you can draw is just that—a circle. Stand at the center of your learning area, with the stang or staff in your hand. Hold the stang with both hands so that you lift the bottom end slightly upward, then move that end around you in a circle as you say:

> *This is the boundary of the circle, around me, above me, and below me; as a sphere is the circle cast and consecrated to aid me in my study of the Craft.*

Envision the flow of blue light from the end of the stang, same as you would if using a knife, creating the circle around you and your work space. Your compact circle may include a chair (and desk or table), a lamp perhaps, along with stang, incense, candle, and cup.

You do not need to call upon the Elementals for such a circle, simply because by now you have drawn a few circles (if you have been following the Manual), and you already make the associations: Air is in the incense smoke, Fire in the candle flame, Earth in the stang or staff, and Water in the cup. When you start making these kinds of associations, you are thinking in magical terms, and the Craft is becoming second nature to you.

When you complete this class, you may honor the divine by raising up the cup before the stang and pouring a dab on the ground (if out

A simple altar, with stang and wreath appropriate to the sabbat or esbat.

of doors). Indoors, you will want to have a libation bowl for this; then you can empty the bowl outside or rinse it in the sink while seeing the drink passing through to the local river or sea. Take a drink from the cup and relax a little. You may want to include a snack of some kind, such as a cupcake or muffin, at the base of the stang with the cup. How fancy or how simple you make your ritual is your choice. I enjoy a piece of multigrain round bread.

When you are refreshed, raise up your open arms before the stang and say:

> *Beings and powers of the visible and invisible, depart*
> *in peace! You aid in my work, whisper in my mind,*
> *and bless me from Otherworld, and there is harmony*
> *between us. My blessings take with you.*
> *The circle is cleared.*

Take up the stang and just as you created the circle, you will now open it by moving in the opposite direction. Envision the blue light drawing back into the stang or staff as you turn around, and say:

> *The circle is open yet the circle remains as its magical*
> *power is drawn back into me.*

Set the stang back in place, cross your arms over your chest, and say:

> *The ceremony is ended. Blessings have been given*
> *and Blessings have been received; may the peace of the*
> *Goddess and the God remain in my heart. So Mote*
> *It Be!*

Snuff out the candle and put your tools away so you can move back into a regular routine.

Consecration of a Statue

Deity Images

Many witches have statues of various deities, but there are some essentials in consecrating statutes and images. These deity images are used as a focal point on altars and in shrines, and some witches will have various statues around the home with special meanings for them in a particular place. Shrines can be placed anywhere: on a desk, in a bookcase, or in some special nook. Modern houses are being built now with shrine rooms in recognition of the multi-cultural religious practices of home buyers. Chinese, Japanese, Hindu, and Buddhist homes have beautiful shrine furniture with statues of the household god or goddess (Kuan Yin is very popular among the Chinese) placed in "houses" that sit at the top of the cabinetry. Incense, flowers, fruit, candles, and paper petitions are arranged around the image. This is also convenient for the practicing witch who desires the same sort of magical environment as a shrine room and such furniture offers. Try looking in Oriental furniture stores for some ideas.

The statues for the Goddess generally allude to her as the lunar aspect of energy or as matter. She is Earth Mother, or Lady of the Moon. The power of the subconscious and her power of regeneration is alluded to in images of the Snake Goddess, Kali, and such. The God statues represent conscious power, solar energy giving life, and the eternal power of energy. He is the Sun God, the Lord of the Animals and the Wildwood, and God of Resurrection. You may even want to use an image that represents both deities in union, such as Shiva Ardhanari or some other androgyne figure (Mercury is often seen as such). This shows the unity or oneness of the male and female aspects of divine power.

A number of New Age and occult supply stores and mail order catalogs have deity images and, surprisingly, so do furniture stores, import stores, and antique shops. Included at the end of this handbook is a listing of mail order places, but JBL has a fine reputation with deity images made from the river banks of the sacred Ganges River of India. Their selection includes not only Hindu and Buddhist deities, but many wonderful images of Greek, Celtic, and Mesopotamian origin including Demeter, Hecate, Lugh, Artemis, Lilith, Astarte, Cerridwen, Cernunnos, Pan, and Dionysus.

One of the most unusual aspects of the Craft is that you can pick and choose your deities. There is no point in trying to relate to an image that does not stir your spirit, so use images that do. If Isis is the mother goddess you relate to, she is happy to welcome your attention. If it is Demeter, Parvati, or Artemis that you feel close to, the same Goddess will gladly receive your attentions and return the favor. The key is that all the goddesses are *The Goddess*. It is *we* who vary, and she graciously acknowledges our differences and embraces all who come to her. The same applies to god images for the same reasons. He, too, will welcome with open arms any who call upon him by any name.

Hollowed Statues

Once you have acquired the statues you want for your shrine or altar, you need to consecrate them. On text page 173 is a ritual for consecrating a tool, but this is not how statues are consecrated. Images have a very potent power in witchcraft because you are drawing energy into the statue to "enliven" it. Look at the statue and see if it is hollow with an opening underneath. Most bronze and brass statues are, and some porcelain ones are as well. Traditionally, the space inside statues is an opening for the purpose of hallowing them.

Use a basic circle (see example in Appendix A of this handbook or text pages 145–152, but substitute the following ritual consecration for a statue where the text shows the Initiation/Rededication ritual). For the following ritual, you will combine in your cauldron herbs that are relevant to the powers you wish to utilize in enlivening the images. Herb suggestions follow on Manual pages 152–153. You can also check text pages 51–59 for the uses of herbs to help in your selection.

Remember to look over the ritual before you begin to be sure you have everything you need—salt, water, cauldron, pentacle, athame, and so forth. Have a bit of each herb in a separate holder on the altar because you address each one before mixing them together. You may want to do this ritual in your kitchen, since there are a lot of materials being used and you will want to use the sink for running water. Otherwise, you will need a basin of spring water.

Place the cauldron on your pentacle. Hold each herb up over the cauldron and state the energy of the herb being drawn upon:

> *I call upon thee* (herb) *to send into my work thy power of* (attribute) *for the consecration and enlivening of this image of* (deity name).

There may be as few as five herbs or as many as thirteen. You only need a dab of each herb. You will use herbs for the deity and for the Elementals as represented by that deity—refer to the listing that follows. Once all are in the cauldron, stir them together with the athame:

> *Through the power of the Goddess and the God* (or use deity names here) *are these herbs blessed for the consecration and enlivening of this image of* (dcity name).

Place the herbs in a small pouch (an unbleached muslin or natural cotton pouch is the best material, because it allows the herbs to "breathe"). If your pouch has drawstrings, wrap the ends around the stuffed bag—otherwise fold the pouch shut. Set the cauldron to one side of the pentacle. Pass the herbal pouch through each of the Elementals:

By Earth you have form (sprinkle with salt),
By Air you have breath (pass through incense smoke),
By Fire you have energy (pass through candle flame),
By Water you have the fluids of life (sprinkle with
  water).

Place the pouch on the pentacle. With the athame in your power hand, raise your open arms overhead to gather in energy:

I call upon the Power of the Lady and the Lord to bless and empower these herbs with their divine essence.

Bring your hands together to hold the knife and bring it down to touch the pouch with the tip. See the energy flow through the blade into the pouch. Set down the athame and place your hands palms down above the pouch:

By Spirit are you charged and enlivened.

Now the image is given spiritual birth through the materials of the Sacred Cow. The Sacred Cow image is found in Hathor, the most ancient goddess of Egypt, portrayed in some statues with the solar disk between her horns. In India today, the gifts of the cow are used to sanctify the deity images and sacred stones in temples, particularly those dedicated to Shiva. There are those who speculate that the cow image came into being because the uterus and the fallopian tubes look like a horned cow's head, which is an interesting idea that may perhaps be used as a point of focus as you continue the ritual.

With the essences of the Divine Cow, who gives of herself in many ways for the lives of others, is this image now blessed.

Carefully hold the statue and rub it all over with soft butter:

With butter are you anointed.

Then rub it over with a soft cheese like a brie, cottage cheese, or use a plain yogurt or sour cream:

With cheese are you fed.

Wash the statue over with about a cup of milk:

With milk are you given the essence of life.

Rinse the statue off with spring water or running water:

With water are you cleansed and purified.

Dry the statue and anoint it with consecration oil.

In the names of the Goddess and the God (or state the names you use) *I consecrate this statue. Let this image of* (Name) *draw* (His/Her) *divine power into my home and into my Craft. Let this image remind me that* (Name) *is always close to me, as I am always close to* (Name).

Pick up the herb bundle and tuck it securely inside the statue. If you are concerned that the bundle may fall out, then you can close off the bottom of the statue with a piece of felt cut to fit and glued along the edges. I have not had a problem with herb bundles falling, even when moving. Usually the curves of the figure are sufficient to hold the bundle in place.

Set the image on the pentacle and cover it completely with a black cloth. Pick up your athame or wand—athame for images of the God and Dual Deity; wand for images of the Goddess—to call the Divine into the statue. Hold the athame or wand upright with your arms raised and open before the covered statue and say:

I call upon thee Elemental Earth, Elemental Air, Elemental Fire, and Elemental Water to bring thy energy and thy power that this image of (deity name) *be made ready for enlivening.*

Bring your hands together to hold the tool and slowly point it toward the statue as you say:

> *Come Great Lady* (Great Lord) *and inhabit this image I have prepared for Thee. Let Thy presence in my life and in my home be a comfort and joy to me.*

Touch the statue with the tip of the tool and feel the power of the divine entering into the image. Leave the statue on the pentacle for grounding and set the tool back on the altar.

Once the statue is energized, you need to secure the power within it. Carefully unveil the statue and set aside the cloth. Verbally welcome the deity by name and place an offering before it such as a cornbread muffin, fruit, or flowers, or you may want to use a dish with food and a small cup with a beverage of some sort. Light an incense such as frankincense on one side of the statue and a white candle on the other side. Let the candle burn for at least an hour.

> *Welcome to my home and my heart, Great Lady/Lord* (Name). *I am blessed by Thy presence, and my blessings I give unto Thee. Let the light of Thy love be with me always.*

After an hour, place the statue where you plan to keep it. Offerings, incense, and candles will change in accordance with your need, the season, the Sabbat, and so forth, because the statue is now a focal point for your practice. Do not feel odd about talking to the image or meditating on it, for this is an ancient practice that strengthens the ties between yourself and the divine.

For statues that have no hollow spaces for an herb bundle, touch the herb pouch to the statue. Lightly anoint the image with a consecration oil, then set the statue on the pentacle and cover it with a black cloth. The herb bundle should also be under the cloth, either under the statue, behind it, or draped against it. Follow the above procedure, but the herb bundle should be kept close to the statue, perhaps in a small covered jar behind the image.

A ritual dedication of a Goddess image incorporates candles and incense; the colors and scents may be changed in accordance with the seasons, the sabbats, and individual needs or purposes.

Porous and Non-hollow Statues

With statues that are made of porous materials, are soft-baked, nonglazed, you may use an alternate method of enlivening. Pass the image through the Elementals, then sprinkle the statue with spring water. When you have mixed your herbs, place them in the pouch and touch this to the statue. Lightly anoint the image with a consecration oil, then set the statue on the pentacle with the herb bundle and cover it with a black cloth.

Using the tool of choice, athame or wand, call the Divine into the image as shown above. Light incense on one side and a candle on the other side. Unveil the image and greet the deity. Light incense on one side of the statue and a white candle on the other side, and place an offering before the Divine.

Consecration Herbs for Deity Images

The term "image" is used because not all deity representations are statues. Some are stones, pieces of wood, pottery, bowls, and pictures. If the image is something that can be consecrated as previously shown, the herbal pouch may be created and placed inside the image, under the image, behind the image, or looped over or around the image. Herbs may consist of stems, roots, and bark, depending on which ones from the following lists are selected and whether or not you are able to get them. For example, you may find there are no alder trees around for alder leaves, but you can get the bark chips at a shop that carries herbs as teas.

The best herbs of course, are those you gather fresh in the light of the Full Moon, but if you are unable to do so, the herbs you buy can be reenergized by exposing them to the moonlight. Stir the herbs up with your fingers and speak to the energies within to awaken and refresh themselves in the light of the Full Moon so that they may be ready to work with you. The choice of herbs for the ritual described is up to the individual, but here is a list of suggested herbs. You only need select a few herbs for your bundle.

Goddess Image

For the Goddess: marjoram, moonwort, elder flower

For Earth: cypress, honeysuckle, jasmine

For Air: anise seed, comfrey, elder wood, eyebright, hazel, lavender, mugwort

For Fire: angelica, celandine, coriander, heliotrope, hyssop, nettle, primrose, rowan

For Water: chamomile, camphor, catnip, geranium, hawthorn, hyacinth, ivy, rose, willow

God Image

For the God: woodruff, yarrow, bergamot

For Earth: cedar, fern, High John the Conqueror, horehound, pine

For Air: acacia, benzoin, mistletoe, nutmeg, thyme, wormwood

For Fire: alder, basil, betony, cinnamon, clove, holly, oak, peppercorn, thistle

For Water: ash, burdock, hops, orris root, yarrow

Unity Image

For Both the Goddess and the God: mullein, dianthus, heather

For Earth: cinquefoil, mandrake, patchouly, sage, slippery elm

For Air: eucalyptus, lemon verbena, mugwort, peppermint, sandalwood, spearmint

For Fire: bay, juniper, marigold, rosemary, rue, saffron, St. John's wort, vervain

For Water: apple, elecampane, heather, meadowsweet, poppy, star anise, shamrock

Select one herb for each category, or several, depending on the associations you are making for them. The five categories echo the Pentagram: four Elementals, with Spirit represented by the deity.

Divine Couples

Pairings for Balance

There are a number of ways of looking at the unity of the Goddess and the God. Together they form the Ultimate Power, but people often prefer to address them individually. As a partnership they express mutual cooperation, balance, trust, and interdependence, but most of all, they express universal love. The Goddess and the God may be seen as the Lady and the Lord; the Moon and the Sun; the Earth and the Sky; Female and Male energies; Matter and Energy.

There are a variety of mythologies used as metaphors in an attempt to make the divine more accessible. Through story-telling we become accustomed to concepts and develop a feel for how The Power interacts. Unfortunately, over time the mythologies have become a tool for usurping one group's deity image for that of a conquering group. The basis behind a lot of the popular Greek mythology and Medieval saint and miracle stories is the undermining of a people's cultural impression of the power of their older deities. Joseph Campbell, in his series of books on *The Masks of God*, shows this process in great detail, as does Robert Graves to some degree in *White Goddess*.

The myths of Shiva and Brahma illustrate the point well when one myth appears to usurp the power of Shiva, ending with Brahma as most powerful, only to be undermined in the next myth by Shiva's greater demonstration of power previously withheld by his extraordinary generosity and imperturbability in such rivalries. These Indian myths are especially interesting, since we know that Shiva dates back some thirty thousand years (yes, 28,000 B.C.E.), whereas Brahma is the newcomer god of Vedic conquerors circa 1250 B.C.E. The older god could not be eliminated, but was accepted into Hinduism. These little details of history always make me giggle—rather like the ancient Dravidians of the Indus Valley saying for Shiva: "When you *know* you are the Cosmic Dancer of the Universe, what do you care about other people's silly myths?"

Underlying a lot of myths that have come down to us is a hidden truth that can be discovered with the understanding of historical events. Thus, the heroic myth of Apollo destroying the python and seizing control of the Delphic Oracle is more realistically a telling of how the invading Hellenes overpowered the priestesses and women warriors defending the Pythagoric Oracle of the Goddess. The priestesses remained, since they were the only ones able to utilize the oracle, but they were placed in subordination to the newly installed priests of Apollo.

Many of the myths reveal episodes in the overthrowing of the Great Goddess religions of settled civilizations by nomadic armies originating in the Ukranian Steppes. Myths are used to redirect the spirituality of the conquered people to accepting their new rulers. There were agricultural communities and successful civilizations where the Lord and the Lady were reverenced as a balance, but these peoples were overrun by another people whose deities reflected their political situation, expressed in hierarchical and male dominant rituals and mythology.

In the older myths, there are a number of matchings of divine beings. There are wedded pairs such as Hera, a Sky Goddess who was "married" to the ruling god of the invaders, Zeus; Aphrodite, goddess of love and beauty, wed to Hephaestus, the divine blacksmith of the gods; and Mesopotamian supreme deities El and Elat. In Celtic myths there are Tailtiu (Teiltui), goddess of the Earth, wed to Eochaid macEire, king of the aboriginal Irish. This is an example of mating a goddess with a mortal king, possibly for his later sacrifice into the land for the benefit of the people. Shiva and Parvati of ancient India have a large number of myths associated with them, but are basically viewed as the ideal couple.

Some myths have love-crossed couples whose tragic affair leads to resurrection or some other expression of the immortality of the soul through the regenerating power of the goddess. Greek Aphrodite and Adonis, Mesopotamian Ishtar and Tammuz, Egyptian Isis and Osiris, and Phrygian Cybele (pronounced KU-bi-lee) and Attis, are all matchings of goddesses with vegetation gods. The god dies—and the myth varies on the cause of death: sometimes by a careless or even deliberate action of the goddess—and the god is resurrected every year through the intervention of the goddess. She is often the cause of death, but is also the source of all life and rebirth.

There are some divine lovers who are not wedded couples, such as Ares and Aphrodite, and a myriad of unions by Zeus (and other

Greek gods) with nymphs, women, and goddesses. A book on various mythologies would be a help if you are looking for a particular situation to address. By calling upon someone in the myth, you are singling out and drawing upon a specific aspect of universal power. This is not necessary for all magics and rituals, but some people may find this a useful practice. It is simply another method of connecting with The Power.

Intuitive Pairings

You can also match couples through intuitive pairings of Dark and Light, similarity of place, and similarity of function. So you could see Celtic Pwyll and Rhiannon as rulers of the Underworld, or Greek Hades and Persephone for the same rulership. But the matchings do not need to fit mythology if your intuitive feelings for the deities forms a link between them and yourself. You could see the horned god Cernunnos matched with the corn goddess Cerridwen, or Lugh, the sun god paired with the earth goddess, Tailtiu, for while another goddess name is used, it is his marriage and descent into the Earth that is celebrated at Lughnassadh. Although the names and stories vary from myth to myth, the elements are the same.

When you consider similarity of place for the goddess and the god, you may want to explore pairings for the earth, the sea, the sky, Faerie, and so forth. The foregoing was an example of Underworld, but for the King and Queen of the Heavens, you might feel attuned to such divine couples as Zeus and Hera, Jupiter and Juno, Isis and Osiris, Odin and Frigg, and so forth. For the Lady and Lord of Faerie, you could think of Titania and Oberon. There are many sea god names to chose from, but sea goddesses are fewer. Sea gods include Poseidon, Lir, Neptune, Oceanus, Nereus, and Njord, while Sea goddesses include Ran, Asherat, Astarte, Ashtoreth, and Ishtar. You could use the generic titles of Lady and Lord of the Seas, or you may want to pair the Celtic

Manannan macLir with Ashtoreth. The intent is the same: addressing the male and female divine as related to the sea.

When working magic, the aspect of The Power being invoked and drawn into your work can be addressed by a particular function. You have the divine couple, with or without names, and you draw attention to the specific aspect you seek to utilize through calling upon them in relation to the function. Thus, you can call upon the God and the Goddess of Fertility, the God and the Goddess of Health, the God and the Goddess of Earthly Power, the God and the Goddess of Creativity, the God and the Goddess of the Hunt (this can include job-hunting or marital partner-hunting as well as hunting of game), and the God and the Goddess of the Harvest. The latter can refer to agriculture or reaping the rewards of your hard work in any field of endeavor.

Whether you use names or not, the image you hold of the desired effect is what drives the magic. The Power does not require identification with a name that may mean one thing to one person and quite another thing to someone else. Where the connection occurs in the Green Craft is within the practitioner. The magics you create, focus, and direct move through you to the outer world. If there are are names that resonate for you, by all means use them, but if you cannot think of what ancient deity represented the sea or the sun; or if you feel a deity name is tied down by the baggage of a mythology created for an obsolete purpose, then use the image in your heart for the function or the placement upon which you are focusing a magical project.

Developing Your Own Pantheon

By exploring some of the myths and legends about the ancient deities you can find which ones give you a feel for the Goddess and the God of the Craft. The aspects and images change, and you may find that you end up with Rhea, Hecate, Shiva, Parvati, Pan, Dionysus, Kuan Yin, Minerva, Artemis, and Cernunnos in your personal pantheon. The impressions these images make within you is what should be your guide, rather than whether or not they are mythically interrelated.

I have heard criticisms over mixing pantheons, but the reality is that all Western mainstream religions have already done that by adopting various gods and goddesses as saints and legendary figures. Even the name "Jesus" is the Greek translation for the Aramaic Isha, which is the Hindu title reserved solely for Shiva. So who is being worshipped? Many books listed in the bibliography of my book, *Dancing Shadows: The Roots of Western Religious Beliefs*,* point to the scrambled beginnings of the major modern religions of the western world.

My point is that you are not mixing pantheons. You are focusing on images of the Great Goddess and the Great God that are found all over the world, and that the drawing of these images into your sphere is personal and direct. How they speak to *you* is what matters, not how anyone else has ever heard them or viewed them. That is the difference between a living and non-living theology—changes are expected.

Some people have a deity who protects the home, other deities for shrines and altars, and call upon yet other deities for a specific goal. When working with different phases of the Moon, there are different aspects of the Goddess to address: Persephone or Diana perhaps for the Maiden (Waxing) Moon; Demeter or Artemis for the Mother (Full) Moon; and Hecate or Cerridwen for the Crone (Dark) Moon. A deity image is simply an aspect of the Divine Power you can focus upon.

---

* *Dancing Shadows* (Llewellyn Publications, 1994) is currently being revised for a proposed new edition, but the first edition may be available in some libraries.

Holy Days: Creating Your Own Calendar of Observances

Wheel of the Year

The most common calendar of witches is one featuring the eight Sabbats. The Quarters are the equinoxes and solstices, while the Cross Quarters are, datewise, the unevenly sectioned traditional points in between. These latter are based upon harvest and planting cycles. Some New Age shops, catalogs, and occult supply shops have Amber K's lovely Wheel of the Year on parchment, suitable for framing. Traditionally, the circle is drawn with eight evenly segmented spaces for the Sabbats, and the witchcraft expression of *the turning of the wheel* refers to the passage through this yearly cycle of eight sabbats. The definition for Quarters and Cross Quarters vary depending upon the tradition. Some see the equinoxes and solstices as the Cross Quarters, others as the Quarters, which is what I prefer.

The other terms used for these eight sections of the Wheel are Lesser Sabbats and Greater Sabbats. Most traditions use the solstices and equinoxes as their Lesser Sabbats, so you end up with a calendar featuring the Lesser Sabbats (Quarters) of Yule, the Winter Solstice (December 21); Ostara, Spring Equinox (March 21); Litha, Summer Solstice (June 21); and Mabon, Autumn Equinox (September 21) interspersed with the Greater Sabbats (Cross-Quarters): Samhain (October 31); Imbolc (February 2); Beltane (May 1); and Lughnassadh (August 1).

The Sabbat Wheel of the Year moves in sequence, beginning at various points depending on your tradition or preference. Modern Western society uses December 31 as the end of the year (Hogmany Eve or the Hag's Eve), and January 1 as the start of the New Year (Hogmany Day or the Hag's Day). The Celts used Samhain, which is modern Halloween. This holiday name translates into All Hallows Eve. Witches will say that this time is when

159

the veil between the worlds is thinnest, but what does that mean? To understand the phrase, you need to follow the life-cycle of the God. He is born at Yule; pursues the Goddess at Ostara; unites with her at Beltane; impregnates her with himself (this same theme was brought into Christianity) at Litha; weds her at Lughnassadh, entering into the Earth; rules Underworld awaiting the Goddess as Crone at Mabon; and at Samhain, the Crone comes to him so he can pass through the Goddess as Tomb to be born of the Goddess as Womb. She transforms into the Goddess as Expectant Mother.

That instant of passage for the God—typically believed to occur at Midnight—is the basis for Hallows. The Lord is totally within the Lady. Darkness resides within Light. Death dwells within Life and becomes New Life, part of the Promise of Resurrection. This is the Great Mystery celebrated all over the pagan world for thousands of years. The partition between what is *hallowed* (holy) afterlife and what is material incarnate life disappears at midnight on All Hallows Eve, and because the partition vanishes, *all* becomes Hallows—the whole world becomes holy for an instant.

The physical world has a moment of grace and union with Otherworld and Underworld. That is why this time was holy and sacred. Although some people attempt to trivialize it in modern times or change it into a Fall Festival of dress-up in a church's basement or community room, the full pagan impact of Samhain is enormously powerful and inspirational. The God moves as we do, through the Goddess, to rebirth. Death is the passage to life, the Crone is the Mother, and the Lord of Shadows is the Lord of Light, and we are reminded that we, too, are immortal.

Samhain celebrates this exact moment of the Lady's transformation from Autumn's Crone to the Mother-to-be of Yule. The Lady is both Crone and Mother through the rest of winter, turning back to maiden after Imbolc. This multiple aspect ability of the Goddess is why she is called Changing and Changeable. The God undergoes transitions or passages in relation to the changing aspects of the Goddess.

Eight Sabbats

- Samhain (October 31) Death/Promise: last harvest; God and Goddess together in Shadowland; veil between the worlds thins; God passes through the Tomb of the Dark Goddess to be born from the Womb of the Mother Goddess

- Yule (December 21) Winter Solstice: rebirth of the Sun; God reborn through the Goddess

- Imbolc (February 2) Purification/Dedication: preparing for the planting of Spring; the Lady recovers from childbirth; Corn Doll in the Bride's Bed

- Ostara (March 21) Spring Equinox: renewal of the Earth; seed planting; God and Goddess influence Nature to reproduce

- Beltane (May 1) Fertility: planting/pollination; animals breed; union of the God and the Goddess

- Litha (June 21) Summer Solstice (also called Midsummer): purification; Fairy Festival; height of Earth's fertility; God impregnates the Goddess with Himself

- Lughnassadh (August 1) Bread: first harvest; God as Willing Sacrifice enters the Earth to give His Life Essence into the grain that supports our lives; God enters Underworld (also called Shadowland)

- Mabon (September 21) Autumn Equinox: second harvest; Thanksgiving; God departed from the Goddess rules in Underworld and awaits Her arrival as Crone

Calendar Days

Every Yuletide in my home includes a calendar for everyone under the Yule tree. One of the projects between Yule and Hogmany is to write into the calendar all the special days. As events of the year move on, the calendar becomes a diary of important highlights such as the first and last day of school for the children, birthdays, anniversaries, graduations, promotions, surgeries, weather notes, concerts, meetings, moves, astrological events like comets, and so on. The calendar for each year is kept, and by picking one up, I can review at a glance all the major events in a year gone by.

For me, the first items placed on the new calendar are always the Sabbats and the Esbats (Full and Dark Moons). I like to label each moon with the title I have for it. There are variations on Moon Names, but this is my listing for the thirteen annual moons and approximate month:

Oak Moon (Yule)   Mead Moon (July)
Wolf Moon (January)   Wort (Herb) Moon (August)
Storm Moon (February)   Barley Moon (August)
Sap Moon (March)   Harvest Moon (September)
Seed Moon (April)   Hunter's Moon (October)
Hare Moon (May)   Snow Moon (November)
Faerie Moon (June)

The labeling of the moons always begins with the Oak Moon being the closest to Yule, and the rest falling in order from there. One month will have two Full Moons—the second one is also known as the Blue Moon, when the power of the Other People can be especially drawn upon.

By starting your calendar labeling with the Oak Moon, you won't get confused as to which moon is which as you progress. There are other names commonly used for the moons, including Wine Moon or Silver Moon for September, Corn Moon for

August, Snow Moon for February, Chaste Moon for March, and Blood Moon for October.

This other moon name for October is used in the Green Craft as is the Blue Moon—only when there actually is one. A Blood Moon occurs on a night when the Full Moon glows bright red. While this often happens in October, it also may be seen in August. An August Blood Moon highlights the passage of the God's blood into the Earth for her fertility. Such a moon on Lughnassadh certainly adds power to the ritual. Blood Moon and Blue Moon are auxiliary names, then, that are descriptive of the moon in any particular month in which they appear. Hence, a Barley Moon could also be a Blood Moon, or the Hunter's Moon could be a Blood Moon.

The portent of the Blood Moon changes with the type of moon. In a Wort Moon, this could be seen as an omen of illness, disease, or plague. In a Barley Moon, the omen might be of senseless war (barley being connected with strong alcoholic drink) or death (for the passing of Lugh). In a Hunter's Moon, the portent is usually of plentiful game, along with a warning not to slaughter more than is needed. In a Harvest Moon, there is an omen of danger to the crops and warning of possible crop failures or famine.

When you find both Esbats and Sabbats occurring on the same day, you may want to perform both rituals together—one after the other. Since magical workings are generally not done on Sabbats, you would want to keep these in the Esbat portion of your ritual.

Picking the rest of your holy days can be quite enlightening as you discover what aspects of the Craft you are most drawn to. There are a number of sources you can use to find out about special days, including a book of days relating to the goddess, magical and witches' almanacs, even the *Witches' Calendar* and *Witches' Datebook* available through Llewellyn Publications. A few examples of these special days are listed on the next eight pages.

Calendar Planner

January

1 Scottish Hogmany Day: Hag's Day

Day of Ishtar (Inanna, Ashtart, Ashtaroth, Ashtoreth, Anat, Astarte, Anaitis, Atar, Isis): Goddess of Love and Battle

3 Nativity of Inanna: Queen of Heaven and Earth; Horned Moon Goddess

5 Scottish Wassail Eve (Twelfth Night, Naming Day): children named; Craft initiates named

6 Celtic Day of the Triple Goddess

Fool's Parade on the Last Day of Yuletide

Lord of the Dance—Shiva beseeched for prosperity, wisdom, a spouse

8 Druid New Year

Macedonian Midwife's Day

9 Festival of Isis: Mother Goddess, Great Goddess, Throne of Egypt

10 Norse Day of Freya, English Plough Day: Earth Goddess invoked

13 Druidic Feast of Brewing

15 Roman Feast of the Ass: saved Vesta, who could only be approached by mothers and Vestal Priestesses

16 French Day of the Queen of the Universe

Festival of Ganesh: God of Success

17 Roman Felicitas: Peace Day for Felicitas, Pax, and Concordia

18 Celtic Day of Danu: Great Mother Goddess

23 Egyptian Day of Hathor: Goddess of Love, Tombs, and the Sky

27 Roman Seed Festival: bless and prepare seeds for planting

February

1 Lesser Eleusinia: Demeter, Persephone, Dionysus (or February 19, 27, or 28)

Month-long festival of Februus: Etruscan Dark Lord of Underworld

2 Imbolc, Lady's Day, Candlemas: Purifications for impending Spring

7 Greek Day of Selene: Moon Goddess

14 Norse Family Festival: modern Valentine's Day

15 Lupercalia (Festival of the Wolf): Pan, fertility, coming Spring

26 Egyptian Day of Nut: Goddess of Healing and Fertility

28 Saxon Cake Day: cakes offered to the God and the Goddess

March

4 Celtic Feast of Rhiannon: Moon Goddess, Underworld Goddess

9 Mother Goddess Day: honoring all Mother Goddesses

11 Great Night of Shiva: vigil and feast for Transcendence

12 Babylonian Feast of Marduk: consort of Bel

14 Egyptian Festival of Au Set: Snake Goddess who wards poverty

Roman Equirria: horse race dedicated to Mars

15–27 Phrygian Festival of Cybele and Attis: Goddess of Earth/Wild Animals and God of Vegetation, Death and Resurrection

17 Roman Liberalia: Women's Maenad festival of Bacchus (Dionysus)

Canaanite Festival of Astarte: Goddess of Love

21 Ostara: Saxon Spring Goddess Easter, Equinox

25 British Lady Day: derived from Ann (Danu) as Crone (Grandmother) and therefore, Mother of the Mother (Ann as the Mother of the Virgin Mary)

26 Slavic Plough Day: Mother Earth can now be ploughed

27 Greek Galaxia: Adoration of Cybele

30 Babylonian Day of Bau: Mother of Ea (the Earth)

April

1 Day of Venus: Goddess of Love and the Hunt

Day of Kali: Dark Mother who liberates

4 Greek Megalesia of Cybele: games dedicated to the Great Mother

5 Roman Day of Fortuna: Goddess of Fate

7 Rumanian Feast of Blajini: "Kindly Ones" (Other People) offerings

8 Day of Mooncakes: dedicated to Goddess Selene

12 Roman Cerelia: games dedicated to Ceres, Goddess of Corn

23 Europe Festival of the Green Man: Spirit of Vegetation and Forests

24 Roman Vinalia Priora: Festival of the First Wine

25 Greek Day of Adonis: God of Vegetation and Resurrection

Roman Robligalia: Corn Mothers (Ceres and Demeter) and Harvest

Various Spring Festivals: dedicated to Herne, Pan, Horned God

28–May 3 Floralia: Festival of Goddess Flora; remembrance of those who have passed into Summerland

30 German Walpurgis Night: May Eve

May

1 Beltane: May Day; Sidhe Day; Festival of Spring and Fertility

4 Celtic/British Festival of Cerridwen and Brigit: Corn Goddesses of Fertility, Healing, and Poets

Celtic Sacred Thorn Tree: veneration of the Moon Tree

8 English Furry Dance: Maid Marian's Morris Dancers welcome Spring

9 Roman Lemuria: Feast honoring the ancestors

11 Irish Old May Eve: Lights for the Fairy Mounds

13 Roman Garland Day: offering garlands to Neptune

18 (Celtic/European) Feast of the Horned God: Greenwood, Hunt, and Animals

21 Dark/Bright Mother Goddesses Day: Kali/Parvati; Hecate/Demeter

28 Thracian Feast of Bendidia: Goddess of the Moon, Underworld, and Secrets (honored by my family for at least four generations)

29 British Oak Apple Day: tree worship and fertility

31 Feast of Stella Maris: Venus as the Star of the Sea

June

    5 Earth Mother Day: good harvests

  13 Celtic Feast of Epona: Horse Goddess

  18 Roman Day of Anna: Goddess Danu to the Celts

  21 Litha: Midsummer's Eve/Summer Solstice; fullness of the year

  23 Celtic Day of the Greenman: Herne, Cernunnos, Lugh
      Day of the Fairy Goddess: Aine, Ana, Anu, Danu

  25 Parvati Praise Day: Women's Festival for Earth Mother

  27 Roman Day of the Lares: Household Deities honored and tended

  29 Shiva Day: Lord of the Dance invoked for blessings

  30 Sumerian Day of Aestas: Corn Goddess

July

    1 Greek Kronia: honoring Kronos (Father Time) and Rhea (Old Mother Nature)

  10 Eng/Ger/Norse Day of Holda, Mother Hulda, Hel: Underworld Goddess

  15 Finnish Day of Rauni: Rowan Tree Goddess

  17 Celtic Feast of Tailtiu: Mother Nature Goddess who fostered Lugh

  19 Egyptian Opet Festival: marriage of Isis and Osiris

  23 Roman Neptunalia: honoring Neptune, God of the Sea

  27 Belgium Procession of the Witches: Festival of Witches

  31 Celtic Oidche Lughnassadh: August Eve; Sun God, Harvest God, Horned God willing sacrifice to become the grain of life

August

1 Lughnassadh: Festival of the Sun God Lugh; Bread Festival; First Harvest

3 Macedonian Day of the Dryads: maiden spirits of woods and water

9 Druid Feast of the Fire Spirits

Roman Vinalia Rustica: wine festival of Venus and Pan

11–13 Celtic Puck Fair: Fertility Festival

18 Roman Feast of the Flowers: celebrating achievements

19 Roman Vinalia: Marriage of Bacchus

20 European Marriage Day of the God and the Goddess

21 Greek Festival of Hecate: to protect the harvest

28 Norse Harvest Festival

September

2 Greek Grape Vine Festival: honoring Ariadne and Dionysus

11 Greater Eleusinian Mysteries: rites of Demeter/Persephone/Hades done every five years (prepare on the 2nd, initiates on the 11th, purifying sea bathing on the 12th, offerings of barley and grain on 13th, "holy basket of Demeter"/Persephone's abduction by Hades on the 14th, torch procession for Demeter's search on the 15th, Holy Night/Initiations show mystery/promise of renewed life on the 16th, games/sports/Feast of Divine Life dedicated to Triple Goddess of Kore-Demeter-Persephone on the 18th, return with earthen jars representing the womb of Demeter on the 19th)

13 Egyptian Lighting the Fire Ceremony: for spirits of the dead

21 Mabon: Fall Equinox, Second Harvest, Harvest Home, Thanksgiving

Norse Winter Finding

23 Babylonian Ishtar's Day: Great Goddess

26 Mesopotamian Day of the Sheepfolds: sacrifice to Goat God Azazel

27 Mesopotamian Day of the Willows: Festival of Astarte

29 Greek Festival of Nemesis: Goddess of Fate

October

2 Druid Feast of the Guardian Spirits

4 Roman Jejunium Cereris: Fast Day for Ceres

5 Rumanian Dionysiad: wine festival

Greek Apaturia: three-day meeting of the clans/receiving new children into the clans/dedication on the last day, called Koureotis

14 Greek Thesmophorus: five-day women's pilgrimage for Aphrodite as Goddess of Genetyllis (childbirth), Demeter as Mother of a beautiful child (Persephone), with revelry the first day, celebration the second, temple of Demeter the third, fast and mourning for Persephone the fourth, and rejoicing the fifth day

18 English Great Horn Fair: Festival of Herne using centuries-old reindeer antlers (black and red), involving Marian/Robin of the Wood fertility themes

24 Druid Feast of the Spirits of the Air

26–Nov. 2 Egyptian Zetesis and Heuresis: search and recovery of Osiris by Isis

31 Celtic Samhain: Hallow's Eve; Last Harvest; New Year, day when the veil between the worlds is thinnest (God enters the Goddess' womb for rebirth, hence the tomb becomes the womb)

November

1 Day of the Banshees: Reign of Celtic Cailleach (a Crone Goddess)

2 Egyptian Festival of Hathor: Mother of the Gods

11 Celtic Lunatishees: Day of the Fairie Sidhe, Old November Day

13 Roman Fontinalia: Feast of Fons, God of Springs

14 Druid Feast of the Musicians

16 Thracian Night of Hecate: Goddess of the Moon, Magic, and Witches

22 Roman Festival of Diana: Goddess of Moon, Hunt, Wilderness; Birth

Night of the Burning Lamps: Shiva (the) Pillar of Light, using oil lamps as symbol of Shiva as the Infinite Light

4th Thursday United States Harvest Home, Thanksgiving

27 Day of Parvati: Mother of the Universe

29 Egyptian Feast of Hathor: as Sekhmet, Lioness and Sun Goddess, the alternate of Bast, the Cat Goddess

December

1 Greek/Roman Day of Pallas Athena/Minerva

3 Roman day of Cybele or Rhea: Great Mother

14–28 Halcyon Days: time of tranquility

17 Roman/Greek Saturnalia begins: festival to Saturn/ Kronos as Harvest and Father Time with His scythe

21 Yule: Winter Solstice

Celtic Alban Arthuan: Return of the Sun God

24 Roman Juvinalia: Saturnalia holiday for children with gifts from Father Time as he departs to make way for Sol Invictus

Celtic/German Nodlaig Eve/Modresnach: Night of the Great Mother

25 Roman Sol Invictus: Saturnalia holiday of Birth of the Invincible Sun

European Feasts of Herne, Frey, Saturn, Dionysus: birth of the God, the Light of the World

Babylonian Birth of the Sun to the Queen of Heaven

26–Jan. 6 Yuletide: festivities include Lord of Misrule; Fool's Parade, and masters serving their workers

31 Scottish Hogmany Eve: Hag's Eve

New Year's Eve

Egyptian Lucky Day of Sekhmet

British Wassail

Palmistry

What to Read

Most of my students are fascinated with the art of palmistry, and I fit it in at the end of the class since it really moves quickly when presented. Palmistry is holistic in the sense that it isn't just the lines in one hand that are read, but both hands as well as their shape, fingers, palm, presence and thickness of mounds, length of fingers, and flexibility of thumb. When the palmist takes your hand, all these subtle messages are being assessed and read, even though the reader may seem to be simply prepping your hand for a look at the lines.

Which hand to read? This is the most-often-asked question. Generally speaking, the *left hand* is the "birth hand" that shows your innate aspects and life's potentials. The *right hand* shows how potential is being used. In a good reading, the palmist will examine both hands, but the hand most often read is the *power hand*—the one that the person having the reading favors. If you are ambidextrous, say so, because there is a lot of flow between both hands in this case.

The easiest way to learn about palmistry is know what the criteria are for interpretations and then apply these to the reading. I have my students start with their own hands. Doing an outline of your hand on a piece of paper and then filling it in from the following listings is part of your assignment for this class.

Remember, many hands do not have a lot of the possible features described, and this too tells you something about the person you are reading. I once read for a young woman whose palm was firm and nearly devoid of lines. The only lines present were the major ones, and these were deeply etched. She was a very direct person, unemotional, methodical, sure of herself and her goals, and she knew that when she married it would be deliberately practical. She vouched for my interpretation, by the way, and told me she was studying to become a Certified Public Accountant. She was engaged to a man she picked for his intelligence and compatibility. They planned to wed after college and open a joint business as CPAs.

Hand Types

Air: long fingers, square palm, many fine lines in palm; expressive, emotionally stable, intellectually curious; writers, teachers, public people, communications

Earth: short fingers, square palm, deeply lined palm; serious, practical, active; manual labors like farming, carpentry, machine operator, business, office, sales

Water: long fingers, rectangular palm, many clear lines in palm; sensitive, creative, quiet studious careers and low pressure occupations like research

Fire: short fingers, rectangular palm, shallow, thin lines; creative, energetic, assertive; artists, customer service

Finger Shapes

Conic: sensitive, impulsive, intuitive

Round: balanced disposition, adapts easily to changes

Square: likes order and regularity, confident, clear-thinking

Spatulate: independent, energetic, action-loving

Mixed: versatility, adaptable, can excel in various occupations

Fingers and Their Lengths

Little (Mercury): communications, business, science, relationships
long: shrewd and clever
short: difficulty with self-expression

Ring (Sun): art, personality, creativity, success, talents
long: imaginative, dreamer, takes chances
short: easily frustrated, prefers solid reality

Middle (Saturn): responsibility, self-direction, introspection, wisdom
long: careful and meticulous in duties
short: holds back on abilities

Index (Jupiter): ambition, self-confidence, sociability, leadership, religion
long: is self-assured, a leader
short: is underconfident, insecure

Thumb (Earth/Human): first joint is will, second joint is logic, third joint is the rhythm of life
long overall: is enterprising
short overall: is practical and loyal

longest joint is most influential; equal lengths show a balance

Mound Locations and Descriptions

Mound of Mercury: beneath little finger; none: lack of business skills, unable to communicate well
well-developed: talent for self-expression, liveliness
highly developed: talkative, garrulous

Mound of Sun: beneath ring finger
none: low energy levels, lack of aesthetic interests or creative pursuits
well-developed: artistic ability, love of beauty, fine arts, culinary arts, etc.
highly developed: extravagant, materialistic, vanity, self-indulgence

Mound of Saturn: beneath middle finger
none: indecisiveness, pessimism, humorlessness
well-developed: independent nature, enjoys solitude as well as companionship, self-awareness, emotional balance, fidelity, prudence
highly developed: self-absorbed

Mound of Jupiter: beneath the index finger
none: low self-esteem, idleness, dislike of authority
well-developed: even temper, assertive, self-assured
highly-developed: can be a strong leader or overbearing, vain, and self-absorbed

Mound of Venus: beneath the thumb—everyone will have this one
weak: delicate health, lack of exuberance and sensitivity
firm and round: compassionate, successful, love of outdoors, vitality
highly-developed: physical energy, sexuality, eat and drink a lot

Mound of Moon: opposite of Mound of Venus—balance of
imagination and reality, subconscious, peace, harmony:
weak or none: totally realistic, no fantasizing
well-developed: good intuition and imagination, strong
nurturer
highly-developed: restlessness, active imagination, creativity

Mound of Mars (+): between Mound of Jupiter and Mound of
Venus—shows assertiveness, ability to overcome obstacles:
weak: quiet and passive nature
well-developed: average courage and aggressiveness
highly-developed: hot tempered, passionate

Mound of Mars (-): between Mound of Mercury and Mound
of Moon—shows determination, resistance
weak: not assertive
well-developed: self-reliance, courage, somewhat stubborn
highly-developed: inflexibility, tendency to cruelty or
violence

Plain of Mars: hollow of the center of the palm
shallow: person tends to be confident
average: person tends to careful
deep: person tends to be more timid

Lines of the Hand

Life: around thumb into palm from Mound of Mars (+)
wide arc: warm and responsive person
shallow: aloof and inhibited
curve ends at Mound of Venus: enjoyment of domestic life
curve ends at Mound of Moon: love of adventure and travel
long, unbroken line: long, healthy life
short, unbroken line: shorter, but healthy life
breaks in line: illnesses or life changes
broken toward the end of line: old age of eighty-five
"M" in hand: the clearer it is, the longer the life

Heart: from edge of palm under Mound of Mercury across
upper palm, shows affection:
clean and strong: has a loving nature
chains: indecision
breaks: a disappointment in love
goes through a circle: temporary separation from a loved one
upswing: instinctive sexuality, physical important in love
straight: romantic imagery important in love
2-3 branches at end: physical, emotional, intellectual balance
chained: freely emotional; may be frequently hurt due to
sensitivity
island (especially by Mound of Jupiter): disappointments;
possible divorce

Head: from edge of palm under Mound of Jupiter across mid-
palm, shows intelligence and interests:
clear and strong: so is the mind
straight across the palm: logical thinker
slight downward curve: likes math or science
sharp downward curve: artistic mind
joined with Life line: close ties to family
reaches the Mound of the Moon: highly imaginative
two-thirds across palm: has average intelligence, influenced
by lines touching it
long line: keen insight, range of intellectual interests
wide gap at Life line: impulsive and impatient
narrow gap at Life line: tentativeness

Heart and Head:
close together: cautiousness, introverted
wide apart: independent, high-spirited, extrovert
longest line rules in love; equal lengths show balance
of both

Destiny/Fate: vertical from base of palm to mounds beneath
the fingers, shows career information, not everybody has
long: active throughout life
unbroken: lots of success

crossed/breaks in line: a setback or change in direction
islands: temporary obstacles
fades away at base of palm: career tends to fade with age
small triangle at base of palm end: quiet, uneventful life
starts high in palm: late career
starts at Mound of Moon: several careers; people involved
starts at Mound of Venus: family important in career
second vertical line: 2nd career
ending: location influences career ending

Health: vertical from base of palm toward Mound of
Mercury, shows the state of health; not everyone has one
presence of line: anxieties and nerves
absence of line: general good health

Uranus: vertical along or within the Mound of Moon, show
psychic power, not everyone has one
presence of line: highly intuitive, psychic, perceptive,
eccentricity is a form of expressiveness
absence of line: normal intuitive powers

Bracelets: along wrist below palm show luck and longevity by
clarity and length of lines
1st line by thumb: health
2nd line: wealth
3rd line: happiness
for women: each line is also a week in a month:
complete ones: how many and which weeks in a month are
high energy
incomplete ones: low energy weeks in a month

Little Lines

Neptune: arc at base of palm, shows health
presence of line: tendency to allergies or addictions
(smoking, drinking, overeating, etc.)
absence of line: nonallergic and not prone to addictions

Children: vertical beneath little finger
count the number to see how many children are probable

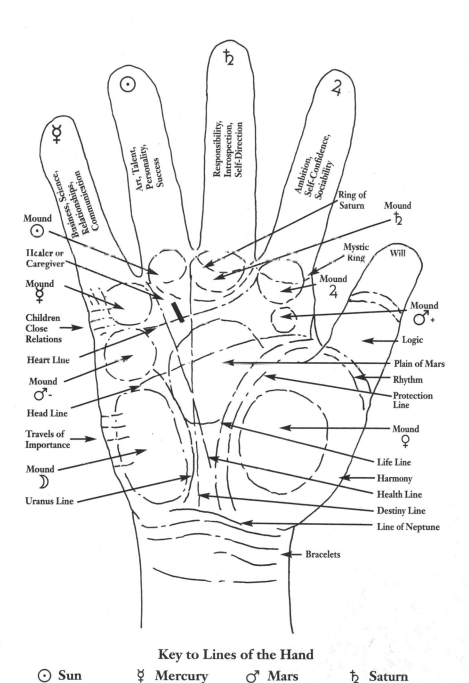

Business, Science, Relationships, Communication

Art, Talent, Personality, Success

Responsibility, Introspection, Self-Direction

Ambition, Self-Confidence, Sociability

Ring of Saturn

Mound ♄

Mystic Ring

Will

Mound ⚴

Mound ☉

Healer or Caregiver

Mound ☿

Children Close Relations

Heart Line

Mound ♂-

Head Line

Travels of Importance

Mound ☽

Uranus Line

Mound ♃

Mound ♂+

Logic

Plain of Mars

Rhythm

Protection Line

Mound ♀

Life Line

Harmony

Health Line

Destiny Line

Line of Neptune

Bracelets

Key to Lines of the Hand

| ☉ Sun | ☿ Mercury | ♂ Mars | ♄ Saturn |
| ☽ Moon | ♀ Venus | ♃ Jupiter | ○ Mounds |

179

Relationships: horizontal lines beneath the little finger
  number of deep friendships or mates
  midway between base of little finger and heart line is age
  thirty-five-ish

Healer: set of vertical lines beneath area between little finger
  and ring finger
  if you have (usually three lines together), person is a healer
  or a caregiver

Travel: horizontal lines at end of palm by Mound of Moon
  deep lines: significant travels
  faint lines: lesser travels
  no lines: travels minimal or are not significantly important
  (vacations)

Circles and Rings

Circle of Venus: arc beneath Mounds of Sun and Saturn
  presence: sensitivity, artistic flair
  Ring of Saturn: arc beneath the ring finger, Mound
  of Saturn
  presence: conservative, sober, enjoys solitude

Mystic Ring: arch beneath the index finger, Mound of Jupiter
  presence: wisdom, able to teach, spiritual discernment and
  authority

Other Marks

  asterisks or triangles: good luck
  cross-hatches on a line: complications
  line breaks and begins anew above or below the former line:
  change
  dots on a line: interruptions
  linked islands on a line: recovering from a crisis
  grid on a line: diffusion of energy
  line ends in a split: adaptability

When it comes to reading a person's palm, I recommend discretion and a complete overview of the hand. Lines can change if a person works at developing areas of limitations. If you lack the ability to be tactful, you could end up hurting people's feelings as well as short-changing them in the reading. Just because someone's hand shows little emotion is not to say the person doesn't love anyone—what is shown is that love is firmly grounded in realistic terms. *Be careful what you do.* The Rules of Conduct still apply.

Assignment

1. Create your own calendar of holy days

2. Draw an outline of your hand on a piece of paper. Draw the lines as carefully as you can to match those in your palm. Now write out the interpretations you can see there. Do you see room for changes? What areas do you want to improve upon? With the palm as your guide, you can create your own learning/development program.

Class 8

Review; Spell Creating & Casting; Types of Magical Spells; Herb Craft; Oils; Basic Candle Magics; Assignment

Review

What are the Rules of Conduct?

1._____

2._____

3._____

4._____

5._____

If you had difficulty remembering the Rules of Conduct, you might want to review Class One where they are introduced and explained. If you had no trouble at all remembering the Rules, good going!

Casting the Learning Circle

This time we will be casting an Elemental Cross circle. You will need a different candle and holder or saucer for each Elemental. The candle for Earth should be green—dark if in fall or winter, light if in spring or summer. The candle for Air should be yellow, and again the shade depends on the season. Fire should have a red candle (or orange candle, but not pink), and the shade can vary from a bright cherry red for spring or summer to a burgundy red for fall or holly red for winter. The candle for Water should be blue, with the shade varying for the season. Light the candles prior to starting.

Have everything you will be using in the center of the place where your circle will be cast. Incense may also be lit and set there. With this circle you are first "setting" the Elementals, rather like monoliths in a paleolithic stone circle, then casting the circle. Your envisionings should be very solid in form, such as four stone pillars with the tops carved with the heads of a bull, eagle, lion, and dolphin, or other Elemental associations. Begin by facing north. With the wand in your power hand, raise your hand and wand straight up, and extend the other hand, palm down, straight out in front of you.

> *I call upon thee Elemental Earth! As we are kith and kin, come and meet with me as I prepare my circle. Secure the boundary of the North and guard against interruptions* (raise the palm of your hand as though doing an imaginary "halt"). *So Mote It Be!*

Drop the hand to your side, bend the elbow of your "wand" arm and bring the wand against your chest, pointing upward, then turn to the opposite Quarter—South. Repeat the process and invocation using the correct Elemental and direction. Turn to the East, do the invocation, turn to the West, and do the invocation. Remain facing West, your wand against your chest, your other hand at your side.

Raise up the wand with your power hand and say:

The circle is cast as a circle of power, anchored by the Elementals and blessed from above and below; inside and without; around and about me. So Mote It Be!

Lower the wand and move West-North-East-South-West in a circle while still standing at the center, envisioning a blue light streaming from the end of the wand, *connecting* the Elementals to the circle. You are back where you were. Set the wand on your altar or table and you are ready to begin the lesson.

When finished with the lesson and any other work you want to do inside this protective circle, have some refreshments for grounding, honoring the Divine as with the Cakes and Wine ritual (text pages 156–157) up to "The circle is now cleared. So mote it be!" Open the circle beginning at the West and moving to the South, then the East, the North, and back to the West with your

Basic altar set-up to use within a learning circle.

wand, envisioning the blue light returning from the boundary of the circle into the wand:

> *The circle is opened, yet the circle remains, its power*
> *flowing around me and through me.*

The Elemental Cross that had anchored the circle is now farewelled. Start at the South, turn to the North, then the West, then the East, and address each Elemental as follows: with the wand in your power hand, upraised, and the palm of your other hand in that "halt" pose. Turn the "halt" hand (slipping or unanchoring), raising it to also clasp the wand.

> *Elemental Fire, thou hast shared thy power with me*
> *and secured my circle as I studied my my Craft. The*
> *lesson of this circle aids me to understand thy power*
> *and our bond, one to another.*

Bring the wand in both hands down to your chest, wand pointing upward. Then open your arms so the wand is in the power hand pointing outward, and the other hand is opened, palm up:

> *The ritual is ended, go in peace.*

Your arms are spread rather like an embrace, so now bring them back to cross on your chest and bow slightly:

> *My blessings take with thee, and thine upon me.*

Snuff the candle and move to the next Elemental, going to Earth, then Water, then Air, repeating the farewell. Put away your tools. Empty your libation from the Cakes and Wine ritual, and touch your palms to the ground to drain off any excessive energy.

This type of casting is performed when in dire need of help or protection, as it calls the Elementals into the circle in a defensive stance. There should be a sense of staunch alliance and security in this kind of circle. An Elemental Cross circle can be used in the event of impending natural upheavals such as tornados, hurricanes, floods, and earthquakes. You can then make your desires known, such as a call for protection of your home.

Spell Creating and Casting

Correspondences for Spell Work

The basic tools for spellworking, discussed in Class One, include wand, ritual knife (athame), cutting knife (bolline), candle, incense, and your Book of Shadows. Additional tools are the cauldron, pentacle, a cup of beverage, bowl of salt, bowl of water, libation bowl, candle snuffer, bell, designators for the Quarters, and Statues, but you do not need all of this to conduct magic. Most of the tools help set the mood and create that altered state where magical power is accessed and directed into manifestation.

Casting a circle is done prior to conducting spellwork. You can have a permanent circle or create one as needed. You can discreetly create a circle when you feel a need for protection from negative energies just by using the forefinger of your power hand. The purpose for the circle during spell work is to contain the energy you are raising until you are ready to let it flow to complete a task. The circle is not a flat spot on the ground around you, but should be envisioned as a sphere that passes through walls and floors, under the ground and through the air above to encapsulate the magic worker. Once the energy is raised and sent, the circle can then be opened.

One of the primary reasons for creating your Book of Shadows, or Spellbook, is to hold your own lists of *correspondences*. This can be handwritten, the traditional method, or typed on the computer. The purpose remains the same—to help keep your practice consistent. The more magic you conduct, the more experience you gain as to what works for you and what does not. Do not be afraid of revising or adding to your correspondences.

The typical listings in a Book of Shadows include herbs and their magical properties (text page 51); incenses and their magical properties (text page 57); colors and their meanings (text page 63); crystals (chapter 8 in *Green Witchcraft II*); symbols (such as runic or ogham) and their use in magic (text page 102/ogham chapter in second book); symbolism in divination (text pages 105–108); days and hours listed with their significance and properties (text pages 67–68).

Symbols present a focus for the magic you are working. With runic and ogham tables, you can use the rune as an alphabet to create inscriptions. Runes are often combined to form magical monograms attuned to a particular goal. The symbols for possessions and wealth can be drawn together as a talisman, for example, and some people will inscribe such monograms onto an appropriate crystal or stone to carry, or onto a candle of the right color for a money spell. The ogham and runes can also be used as individual symbols for their magical meaning. Many people develop their own symbols, such as hearts for love and dollar signs for money.

A list of symbolism is different from one of symbols as this involves images of visual divination such as might appear in tea leaves, candle wax after a spell, clouds, smoke, or dreams (text pages 105–108).

Timing of Spells

With many spells, timing is very important. The phase of the moon is one the major criteria for when to conduct certain types of spells. If the need is urgent, the spell can be crafted to incorporate the type of moon currently available. The moon phases are the new crescent waxing moon, called the Maiden; the full moon, called the Mother, and the old crescent waning moon, called the Crone. There is also the dark moon, which is the hidden face of the Goddess, or the mystic moon.

Just as the various phases of the moon affect tides, they aid the energy flow to particular tasks. Thus, the waxing moon of the

Maiden is the best time for magics dealing with new beginnings or developing works. This is when you do spells for gaining wealth, happiness, a new job, and so forth. The Full Moon of the Mother is the best time for spells of completion and for honoring energies and spirits. This is the most often celebrated Esbat (not all witches celebrate dark moon Esbats). The Full Moon is when you do magics you envision as completed. Often a spell might start a few days before the Full Moon so that by ritually moving a candle or burning it an hour each day until the full moon, you can envision progress on the desired goal and completion on the full moon. Then you no longer work on that spell, but see it as done.

The waning moon of the Crone is best used for magical work involving banishings, purgings, or exorcisms. This is when you get rid of bad habits or banish poverty, for example. The Dark Moon is good for divination, dark power rituals, and spiritual meditations.

Planetary and celestial arrangements can be factored into the timing of your spells if you are so inclined. These include monthly astrological signs, planetary movement in the signs and houses of the Zodiac, planetary inter-relationships (conjunctions, trines, squares, etc.), passing comets, meteor showers, and solar storms. For this, an astrological planner, almanac, or calendar is most useful. General associations with the celestial bodies are:

Sun: individuality, pride, display, success, honors, energy, power

Moon: personality, sensitivity, emotions, desires, start/end of cycles, projects, intuition, contentment

Mars: dynamic energy, aggressiveness, willpower, sex drive, initiative

Mercury: communication, skill, agility, sensory impressions, thinking, learning

Jupiter: optimism, opportunity, health, expansion, finances, wealth, idealism, justice

Venus: sociability, love, friendships, emotions, artistry, values, money, luxuries

Saturn: ambition, structure, realism, self-preservation, self-control, restrictions/freedom, business, materiality

Neptune: occultism, subconscious, psychic energy, spirit, otherworldly, idealism, creativity, illusion

Uranus: sudden and unpredictable changes, tensions, news, originality, knowledge, innovation, divination,

Pluto: transformation, sex, death, rebirth, the soul, evolution, Underworld, extremes, spirituality, life cycle free from bondage

Magic may be timed according to the most propitious hour of the day or night. The planetary tables are discussed on text page 68, but the easiest thing to do is pick up a copy of *Llewellyn's Magical Almanac* for any year. The table is neatly printed out by sunrise and sunset hours, and you can copy it or cut it out and glue it into your Book of Shadows. You can time your spells for an hour that is conveniently situated and ruled by the planetary sign conducive to your purpose.

Just as each hour of the day has a representative planet, so does each day of the week (text pages 67–68):

Sunday—Sun (power; Self; fortune; hopes; spirit)

Monday—Moon (intuition; divination; family; emotion)

Tuesday—Mars (energy; courage; contests; matrimony)

Wednesday—Mercury (communication; reason; skill; money)

Thursday—Jupiter (honor; riches; law; health)

Friday—Venus (love; friends; social; arts; pleasure)

Saturday—Saturn (discipline; secrets; protection; life)

You can optimize the energy of your spell, then, by picking the appropriate moon phase, the appropriate day, and the appropriate hour in which to conduct your magic. Add the right herbs, color of candles, and you are ready. These all come straight out of your Book of Shadows, which is rather like a menu from which you pick selections for each course of the meal as you compose the interacting components of your spell.

The number of the hour is another factor that can be utilized in spell creating. The basis lies in numerology, and if you find astrology too much trouble to deal with, the numbers work very well:

1 the letters A, J, S; Sun; Fire; Developing the Self, the All, Beginning and Ending; Wholeness and Unity

2 the letters B, K, T; Moon; Water; Sensitivity and Personality, Truth, Blessing, Duality; Balance

3 the letters C, L, U; Jupiter; Fire; Health and Opportunity, Triads and Triple Aspects; Career

4 the letters D, M, V; Uranus; Air; Divination & Knowledge, Quarters, Firmness, Strength; Foundations

5 the letters E, N, W; Mercury; Air; Communication, five-fold Aspect of Pentagram (four Elementals + Spirit); Fulfillment

6 the letters F, O, X; Venus; Earth; Sociability and Emotions, Unity of Triple Goddess and Triple God, Magnetism, Cats; Decisions

7 the letters G, P, Y; Neptune; Water; Sub-conscious, Intuition, Psychic Power, Mysticism, Dual Triads as a Unity; Change

8 the letters H, Q, Z; Saturn; Earth; Freedom, Dual Foundations, Material and Spiritual Worlds, Law, Self-discipline; Travel/News

9 the letters I, R; Mars; Fire; Aggression, Energy, New Path, Immortality, Indestructible; Binding to Completion

The digits of larger numbers are added until you get to the base number: 12 is 1 + 2 = 3; 22 is 2 + 2 = 4, so if the day of the week is

15, you could see it as the meaning applied to the number 6; if the spell is conducted in the third hour after sunset, you can focus on the value for that number (sunset at 6 P.M., spell at 9 P.M. for energy). The two-digit numbers may be used for mystical value, the most popular being 13. This it the perfect number of All (1) and Trinity (3), thus, the Universe. Other numbers are 10 for completion, 12 for the even dozens and relation to Faerie magics, and multiples like 11, 22, 33, 44, and so forth for double emphasis of the main number. Sometimes the doubles are read as 2 by 2 or 3 by 3, etc. for a balance of the value of the number. Triples are used for bindings, and quadruples are used for squaring and setting—making the value of the number a foundation for a spell.

Much of Green Witchcraft is more attuned to the moon and the sun rather than the planetary arrangements, but I offer the astrological information simply because it is there, should you be inclined to use it, and because I sometimes incorporate it in my own practice. The numerological information is often used in the Green Craft. You can time your magic then according to moon phase, hour of the day, day of the week, and the numbers of the date. Long-range planning can include the solar phase (season), comets, meteor showers, and so forth. For timing using the planetary hours guide, all you need to find out is when sunrise and sunset occur for any given day in your location. You can find this information in the daily newspaper and also on the weather channel.

As an example of how you could time a spell, let us say you want to increase money flow to you. The day of the week for riches is Thursday, ruled by Jupiter. Jupiter on Thursdays rules the first and eighth hour after sunrise and the third and tenth hour after sunset. The number three is a Jupiter number, so for triple potency, you would want to use a Thursday, the third hour after sunset, during a waxing moon to perform a money spell. Say the sun sets at 6 P.M., the spell is conducted at 9 P.M., and you include in your focus the energy and power of the number 9 (which is 3 x 3, and this is often used as a chanting method of binding a spell to completion). Now your timing is set for optimum results.

Preparation for Spellwork

Once you know what kind of spell you want, and have determined when the best time to perform the ritual is, you need to outline what exactly you plan to do. I recommend using notecards, which you can later file (a recipe box works well for this), subdivided by types of spells, chants, invocations, and blessings. You could also detail each spell in your Book of Shadows or Spellbook. The Spellbook can become something of a jumble over the years, but since you use it constantly, it will have a cozy feel of familiarity to you. If you do have trouble locating your spells, you can always tab the book by spells or insert an index page that you can add to and change as the list grows. The front list of the spells can be alphabetical by topic, with the page number of the spell next to it.

Consider all the details you will need in a spell. List the supplies, the symbols you will inscribe or otherwise use, chants, and step by step procedure. There are some examples of spells on text pages 133–138. Remember to change some aspect of any spell you copy from someone else. This *must* be done to make the spell *yours*. A lot of the grimoires have spells in them that contain a deliberately misleading element. The idea was that only someone who knows what the correlations are can spot the error and correct it, thus making the spell personalized. So when you formulate your timing, for example, you may come up with something different from what another person's spell suggests. You could substitute ingredients, inscriptions, and technique while still incorporating many of the offered details into your own spell.

Once you know what you are doing, when, and with what procedure, you need to prepare the tools and materials in advance to conducting the spell. Purify yourself and the working space. Pick out the incense you want for your circle: stick, cone, powdered, resin, or herbal. With powdered, resin, and herbal incenses, you need a heat-proof container and charcoal blocks. A roll of these small blocks can be found in most variety and gift shops, and anywhere else that incense is sold. Begin with dropping a small amount of the powder, resin, or herbs onto the lit charcoal and the smoke should be released. You can add more incense as desired. Dragon's blood resin adds power to spellwork and yet has a delicious scent. Frankincense and myrrh are other resins traditionally used and have a very "churchy" aroma. Mixed blends of powdered incense are used according to their associations (text page 57–58), as are herbs (text pages 51–56). Charcoal eats up oxygen, so using these blocks requires adequate ventilation. If you feel dizzy or headachy, you need more air.

Now you are ready to create the circle and make your invocations. You may hold an observance such as an Esbat along with spellwork, or you may want a separate ritual just for the spell. In either case, you will raise and then direct that energy to carrying out the goal of the spell. Earth, or ground the residual power by touching the floor or ground with the palms of your hands and envisioning the excess energy draining out. Take some refreshment, do your parting or farewells, open the circle, and put away your tools.

Energy Raising, Focusing, Directing, and Sending

When it comes to creating your spell, you need to identify the purpose. Sometimes it is easy to confuse the outcome with the purpose, but if you delineate to yourself what it is that you want to accomplish, and feel it, then your work will be directed to the purpose of the spell. Suppose, for example, that you merely like someone, but that person appears to be very dependent on you. You want your independence, but don't want to hurt anyone's feelings. To do a spell to find a compatible partner for your friend would accomplish the outcome of relieving you of feeling responsible for this person. But the real problem is that you *do* feel responsible, not that you need to be doing spells involving people who have not asked for them. The true purpose of the spell is to free yourself from the burden of unwanted emotional ties to this person. That makes the spell for you and addresses your feelings about the situation.

Now that the purpose of the spell is known, you can focus on achieving the desired outcome. Use your list of correspondences to construct the spell according to the associations of the topics (herbs, colors, days, hours, etc.) Have a single word/image in mind to state when energy is raised so that you can send it out at the end of the spell—perhaps something like "freedom." You can raise energy with dance, breathing style, and chanting. A chant, repeated over and over with a building of focus and breathing can be used to raise energy and enhance a spell. Most witches compose their own simple rhymes or chants that maintain a beat or rhythm.

Once you feel the raised energy is at a peak, use the single word you have already chosen to send the energy to accomplish the task. While a short phrase can also be used, I believe you dissipate some of the power raised by taking too long to explain where the energy is going and what it is accomplishing. Setting up your materials so that you can use your hands to point the way for the spell may help for spells involving specific directions. If you want your magic to go to New York City, and you live in Illinois, as you end of the spell direct it with your hands motioning to the east. Then see the spell as successfully completed, ground, and have some refreshment.

Another method of raising energy is to chant the traditional Witch's Rune found on the next page.

Darksome night and shining moon
East, then South, then West, then North
Harken to the Witches' Rune
Here I come to call thee forth
Earth and Water, Air and Fire
Wand and pentacle and sword
Work ye unto my desire
Hearken ye unto my word
Cord and censer, scourge and knife
Powers of the Witches' blade
Awaken all ye unto life
Come ye as the charm is made.

Queen of heaven, Queen of hell,
Horned Hunter of the night
Lend your power unto my spell
And work my will by magic rite
By all the power of land and sea
By all the might of moon and sun
As I do will, so mote it be
Chant the spell and be it done
Eko, Eko Azarak
Eko, Eko Zamilak
Eko, Eko Cernunnos
Eko, Eko Aradia (repeat the Ekos until energy is
raised and ready to release).

This chant is often used in conjunction with dancing around the circle, giving you the energy of the chant as well as of the dance. You could also repeat the phrases that especially appeal to you until you are ready to send the energy. The rune itself is actually a combination of ceremonialism and the Gardnerian Tradition. Witches do not recognize "heaven" and "hell," except as the Universe and Underworld or Shadowland. The scourge is also not used in all Traditions, and while today it is generally made of soft materials, the original version (per the murals at Pompeii's House of Mysteries and flagellate tradition) was intended to draw blood. The word "eko" can be traced into history as a Medieval misinterpretation of the cry of the ancient Bacchantes (maenads) of Bacchus (Dionysus), "Evoa," meaning "Thou art invoked."

Included in this Rune are *names of power*, which may be used if they work for you. These names come from the books called grimoires, written by ceremonial magicians of the twelfth century onward. The names come from a variety of sources, including ceremonial lists of angels, demons, spirits, powers, and more. There are names that are supposed to represent planetary, Olympic, and elemental spirits, but many names were simply made up in a frenzy of power-raising by a magician speaking in tongues. The *iel* endings to names give them a connection with Faerie, Otherworld, or Heaven. El is also the most ancient word for the Divine, found in ancient Mesopotamia, as endings to the names of ancient deities and nature spirits, and used as the Hebrew word for "God" (*Beth-el* = House of God).

From the perspective of the Green Witch, the use of the Runes' names of power combines Pagan and Christian deity concepts—two diverse deity images for the Lord and the Lady—which lessens the impact. The Rune, however, can be altered to fit your personal viewpoint and spiritual path, invoking the deities and powers you relate to.

Many other names of power are the ancient deities transformed into mostly into demons (Astaroth, Asamodeus, Asmoday) or into angels and spirits. Other names are Latinized deities or words used as nouns such as "wisdom" is the name Hagenti; Stolas is herbs and stone (particularly the standing stones found all over Europe and accepted as holding occult power). A few sample names of power are: Zazel, Agiel, Yophiel, Agares, Paimon, Zagan, Andrealphus, Abrac, Beleth, Morax, Orias, Ose (which I especially enjoy since this was my great-aunt's name and she was strong-willed, yet sweet-tempered), and Hagenti.

Types of Magical Spells

Type of Spell Defined by Purpose

Spells can be created for a variety of reasons. One of the most common purposes is to draw something to the person casting the spell. Money spells, love spells, spells for healing, and so forth are all examples of drawing spells. In this type, you are filling a need, bringing something positive into your life. The attraction power is enhanced with timing, appropriate herbs, symbols, colors, and the wording you create for your spell. Your focus is identified and stated, and the raised energy is used to pull the necessary positive energies to you.

But spells can also be used to repel, or cast away what is unwanted. This type of spell may be a banishing or exorcism. When you need money, for example, and the moon phase is the Crone's, you could focus your spell as banishing poverty, want, or unemployment. If you feel you are surrounded by negative energy and depression, you can formulate your spell to repel these energies, then draw in positive, optimistic energies.

Where you feel that there is negative energy being directed towards you for whatever reason, you can respond with a spell of containment, deflection, or reflection. These kinds of spells are more fully discussed in *Green Witchcraft II*, but basically, the first type of spell would be crafted to contain the negative energy within the field of the sender. The result here would be that the energy being generated by someone through anger or some other such motivation will be unable to escape the person's own energy field. Deflection spells dissipate negative energies that are directed toward you. The witch's bottle with broken glass, mirror shards, pins, nails, thorns, and other sharp objects can be used as part of a deflection spell that goes into action when you bury the bottle in your yard. But before you bury it, you need to create a spell, raise the energy, focus and send the energy into the bottle. Reflection spells are protective to the spellcaster, with the negative energies being directed to you doing an "about-face" and affecting the original sender. This is a "return to sender" spell where the energies are not disbursed randomly nor prevented from escaping a person's auric field, but turned around to ricochet back to the sender. The sender then receives the brunt of his/her own negative forces.

In all that you do, be sure you are harming none. In other words, you are not initiating negative magic toward a person. Instead, reflection magic returns what has been sent back to the original sender. Deflection magic diffuses and disperses negative energies, while containment magic restricts negative energies to the sphere of origin.

Type of Spell Defined by Method

There are four basic types of spells defined by method. One of the most familiar is comparative magic. With this type of spell, you draw a connection between the objects used in the spell or charm and the focus of the spell or charm. An example of this is creating an Elemental Bottle to enhance your connection between the Elementals and yourself (the spell is in *Green Witchcraft II*). Comparative magic is demonstrated with the spell concept of *"this represents that."* You could plant a seed as part of a spell and say, "as this flower grows, so shall my wealth (friendships, etc.) grow."

Sympathetic magic is another commonly used type of spell. Here the witch will visualize one object as *being* another object which is the actual focus of the spell. For example, poppets and candle burning spells using seals or sigils are forms of sympathetic magic. Often the spell will include something belonging to the object of the spell—especially in the older style love/attraction spells. This is the concept of *"this is that."* A piece of paper or cloth is seen as "this is (name X), burning with love for me" or "this is my pet coming home to me." The item could be burned, or in the second instance moved closer to something representing your home.

Directive magic is also commonly used and is simply the raising of energy, focusing it on a goal, directing the energy, and releasing it to accomplish the goal. Almost all candle-burning magics are of this type. The basic concept here is *"let the energies of this affect that."* You can be directing energy to enhance your health, to draw money, to find a job, and so forth.

The last type of spell is one that is rightly used only with extreme care and need; it is called *transference magic*. With this type of spell, you are moving a negative or detrimental energy from out of a person and into something else to heal the person. This spell will only work with the consent of the recipient, which generally weakens and/or dies. The concept in this type of spell is *"let this take on the harmful energie of that."* An example of this type of spell would be the transferring of an illness from a person into a plant. The visualization would be that as the plant withers, the person heals.

The Rules of Conduct, "Be careful what you do," and "Do not use The Power to hurt another because what is sent comes back," must be heeded. All living entities, including plants and animals, are able to communicate to the witch whether or not they are willing to help. Indeed, these living things usually suggest the transfer, often from love or devotion, or as a chance to cleanse their personal auras or to improve themselves spiritually. Such a gift is priceless, and can only be accepted with reverence and love.

If you attempt this kind of magic without the consent of the recipient you will draw the energy directly to you. If the recipient dies, you could additionally draw the energy of the recipient in a spirit of hostility, so you would be doubly affected. Your own auric field would be diminished by this act as well, and thus you would be triply affected. This is the only time in the Green Craft where the Rule of Conduct: "Do not use The Power to hurt another because what is sent comes back," is increased. All energy must be moved with purpose to achieve this three-fold return. If the recipient forgives you, the return is two-fold rather than three-fold.

The prime example of this type of spell is when a mother draws to herself any negative energies that may surround her child, because she is stronger and more aware, and perhaps she will be able to dissipate those negative energies. Her actions work through the strength of her love for her child.

A devoted family pet may volunteer to take on a deleterious energy to protect a family member. The spell moves the adverse energies from the family member to the pet. The pet may be better equipped than the person to handle this energy, or the pet may succumb to the adverse energy. My mother felt that much of this kind of energy is generated unconsciously by people who are envious or jealous of someone else's family, happiness, or good fortune.

Herb Crafts

Herb Gardening

When you work with herbs, remember to refer to your list of herbal symbols. Try to keep your practice consistent and the energies being called upon will be clear to you. Growing your own herbs gives you maximum control over the cultivation and harvesting of herbs for magical intent. You can plant in your garden the herbs you tend to use most of all.

While most seed packets and advisories recommend growing herbs in full sunlight, this really depends on where you are. In places like Florida, Texas, the Southwestern states, and the desert areas of California, you will achieve better results if you plant your herbs on the north side of your yard. Placing an herb garden under a protective shade tree will keep the plants from withering in the blazing heat of the sun. While sunlight is needed, the burning heat can be hard on herbs.

Watering varies with the herbs, but a soaker hose placed in the ground passing among the herbs works very well. Most herbs are great self-seeders, and it always amazes me how far-flung seedlings can be from their parent plant. I have had heather turn up in the brick walkway and thrive there, and bronze fennel pop up in the opposite end of the garden. Herbs like St. John's wort and pennyroyal (wards fleas!) will spread as a ground cover if given the chance, so there are some herbs more suited to large containers. Betony will take over your garden and is very difficult to remove. This plant will multiply throughout the garden by sending new shoots up from its spreading roots. Mint will do this above ground and below ground, so it too is better suited to growing in a large container.

There are a lot of beautiful, decorative, and old-fashioned styled pots that hold a substantial amount of soil. While some plants do thrive in sandy soil, herbs are basically what many people call weeds, and they will grow just about anywhere because that is part of their hardy nature. You can grow plants like rosemary (which can become a large shrub) and artemisia (another large, spreading shrub) in pots, or you can place them in the garden according to size. Look for herb books in the garden section of the bookstore or library for ideas on how you want to arrange your own garden.

Mugwort will spread rather low to the ground and send up tall stalks, but grows better in temperate climates. When you pick a stalk of mugwort, you can shape it into a circle and wrap the end around itself and the circle will hold. This is a good herb to place in your magic area, or to set on top of your crystal ball.

Spices such as marjoram, thyme, dill, chives, basil, and coriander will grow in clumps as long as you nip off their flower buds. Once they flower, these plants tend to decline. Borage and comfrey will grow larger and larger, rather like cauliflower—low but spread out.

When you gather your herbs, be sure to let them know in advance what you want: "I need your help in a spell," or "I need the power of your flavor in my (meal)." Give the plant your blessing, look at it carefully to see what part of itself the herb is willing to give to you. This is an instance where your intuitive powers come into play. You may want to leave a gift for the plant, depending on the use you have for the piece you are taking. The gift could be anything from a cup of water, to a crushed eggshell (my mother used these a lot, especially for the home protection plants called "Hen and Chicks"), to a shiny coin stuck in the ground. Even coffee grounds make a gift, since they represent power and strength. This is a kind of reciprocal magic between you and the herb.

Magical Teas

On text pages 110–114 there is information on divination with tea leaves, using the power of teas as part of your magical preparations, and a few examples of tea recipes. How to make a good cup of tea is described on text page 111. Another method for making magical teas is to use an automatic hot tea maker. With this device, you place a filter inside a basket, drop in loose tea to suit, put water in the container, set the pot on the hot plate under the drip, set the strength of the tea, and turn it on. It works like an automatic drip coffee maker, and you end up with a delicious pot of tea made from the teas and herbs of your choice. You can place tea bags in the drip basket; in that case do not use the filter. With the automatic tea maker you will not have leaves to read, so if divination is what you have in mind, loose tea in a pot is the better choice.

I generally use a black tea base for the symbolism of strength. The black tea increases or enhances the magical power of the herbs. You might want to try some of the tea recipes in the text. Create your own chants for mixing the teas based on the symbolism of the herbs being used and the purpose of your tea. One example is for a recipe for Faerie (Fairy) tea, used in a Companion Quest ritual (*Green Witchcraft II*, Chapter Four) and good for Midsummer (Litha) and when conducting Faerie or Sidhe magics:

Fairy Tea

Combine in a teapot:

3	tsp	black tea
½	tsp	chamomile
1	tsp	dandelion root
½	tsp	elder flower
½	tsp	hops
½	tsp	mugwort
½	tsp	raspberry leaf
1½	tsp	rose hips

saying as you drop the herbs into the pot or filter basket:

Black for power, apple of night, root of the sun, Lady's blessing, Lord's leap for joy, then between the worlds, to Fairy bramble, with token of love, brewed to bring Fair Ones close to me.

If not using an automatic tea maker, boil water in a kettle and add to a teapot that was warmed with a bit of hot water before the tea leaves and herbs were put in. Let steep for five minutes. Warm a second teapot by swirling inside it more hot water from the kettle. Pour out the water and strain the brewed tea into this warmed pot. Add to taste in your teacup whatever sweetener and milk you like. You may want to have something to eat such as cookies or tea biscuits (Scottish shortbread is very good and can be found in most supermarkets), or other tea snack. This can be part of your Cakes and Wine ritual toward the end of your spellwork, or you can use it to set the mood prior to your Faerie magics.

External Magical Uses for Herbs

Herbs have traditionally been used for various types of cleansings. By mixing an herb having the properties of cleansing with spring water, you can empower the water for washing your tools and altar. Herbs can be hung in bundles around the house to keep the atmosphere fresh and attract beneficial energies while repelling negative energies. You can asperge your sacred space with a sprig of purple heather dipped in holy water saved from a Sabbat or Esbat. This refreshes and revitalizes an area. A house blessing may be conducted by asperging each room, censing each room, and sprinkling the doorways to the house.

Protections and Invitations for Desired Vibrations/entities

A number of herbal crafts are designed to protect the home and/or attract positive energies or protective spiritual entities. A solar wheel can represent power and protection of the God in your home. Instructions are on text page 227. A wreath of mugwort, already described, can be placed in areas where you practice divination and it can also be used for protection. Mixed herbal wreaths look beautiful on the front door, but also serve to screen out negative energies. You can select herbs from the text listing to be used in the bath before a ritual so you can draw upon the powers of the herbal energies. And of course, herbs have been used in cooking for many millennia. Think in terms of the magical meanings of herbs when you add them to your meals: rosemary, marjoram, thyme, sage, basil, and parsley are excellent additives to chicken, pot roast, soups, and stews.

Herbs may be also be used in dream pillows and herbal bags. Choose the color of the cloth to define purpose of the pillow or bag, then select your herbs from list of correspondences. Decorate the bag as you wish, with the idea of enhancing magic or visual image. When the pillow or bag is finished, dedicate it to the purpose for which it was created in a ritual (see Consecration of a

Tool, text page 173 for some ideas). The basic point in your ritual will be to dedicate the pillow or bag to a purpose, passing it through the Elementals for their power, and calling upon the Lady and the Lord for their blessing upon it.

Dream pillows are normally placed under the pillow at night, typically to draw dreams of divination or enhance memory of dreams. You can also place a dream pillow under the mattress sheet to keep it in place. Herbal bags or pouches are more often carried in the purse or pocket either for protection or to attract money; placed somewhere in the car (under the floor mat, in the glove compartment) for protection; or hung in an appropriate place such as in a window of your house, from the interior rear-view mirror of a car, or over a doorway. You can also make four pouches and bury them at the four corners of your property or place them behind the furniture or in a vase or other inconspicuous place in the four corners of room, apartment, or home for protection and attraction of positive energies.

Try creating your own dream pillow. Look over the herbs listed in the text and select the ones you want to use. Choose the color of the material and thread based on the purpose as related to the color list. Think on the magical intent as you work and how the time of day and phase of the moon relate to your purpose. Consecrate the pillow by stating the purpose of the pillow, passing it through the symbols of the Elementals, and invoking the blessing of the Lady and the Lord. Then set it on the pentacle on your altar, with a lit white candle and incense at either side. After an hour, it is ready to use.

Oils

Herbs in Oils

Herbal scented oils (refer to text pages 128–130) stimulate the senses and help to open the awareness of an individual while linking the herbal essence with the person to assist the practitioner in reaching an altered state for magical work. These oils infuse the power of the herbs into whatever they touch, so there are a variety of uses for them, depending on which herbs are in the oils. Oils may be used for anointing yourself and others in the circle. They are used for consecrating tools and spellworking materials, dressing candles and ritual objects for magical work, and as an aid to astral projection and meditation. An herbal scented oil may be used in the consecration of a box to keep magic tools and supplies inside, and to aid in the empowerment of objects used in a spell.

Making ritual oils does not have to be complicated. There are a lot of ready-made oils available in health food stores, occult supply shops, catalogs, and even gift shops. To make your own, add ground herbs to a base of spring water, or an oil such as sunflower or safflower. Next, add a few drops of essential oils. Bottle and store away from light. Try several different combinations and see what you can create.

Types of Magical Oils

Oils have numerous functions in witchcraft. Anointing oil is used during the rituals of Sabbats and Esbats to mark a symbolic design in a circle on the forehead (the psychic center of the "Third Eye") of the practitioner and anyone entering the circle. Consecration oil is used as part of the ritual for dedicating Craft tools. Altar Oil is used to prepare the altar for a particular ritual and may also be sprinkled with a sprig appropriate for the season, such as white heather at Imbolc, wheat at Lughnassadh, holly, pine, or mistletoe at Yule.

Blessing Oil is mainly used in conjunction with a Rite of Passage, such as Presentations, Namings, Handfastings, and Passings, but it can also be used in place of an anointing oil for welcoming a newcomer into the circle or for an initiation ritual. Cleansing Oil is used to revitalize and refresh an area or object, purging it of negativity that may have built up through unwanted contacts, prior inhabitation or possession, and unwanted handling by someone else. It is particularly beneficial in the event of an unwelcomed visitor or quarrels. For asperging a large area or one with furniture, a base of spring water rather than oil might be preferable to avoid accidental spotting.

Astral Projection Oil is used to help induce an altered state of awareness conducive to astral travel. Some older recipes include poisonous herbs such as belladonna, whose toxic effect may inspire hallucinations. The risk of serious injury or death is simply too great for this kind of use, and other recipes are just as effective. The point in astral travel is *not* to hallucinate, but to leave your body. This is not an hallucination but a spiritual movement that can be brought on by proper preparation and practice. One recipe is on text page 129.

When applying oils, there are a number of commonly used symbolic designs you can draw with a finger of the power hand. These designs could be placed on the forehead when entering the circle, on a tool, or on an object. The pentagram is a five-pointed, interlaced star, and for the ritual magic of those traditions with a ceremonial influence, the starting and ending point signifies "summoning" or "banishing" and an Elemental or Spirit. If you are consistent in this type of design drawing, then the starting point will become connected in your mind with that type of feature and will work in that manner. Otherwise, the starting point is not significant, and the pentacle will still work for you.

The solar cross is an equal arm cross representative of the God, especially as the Sun God, or the Invincible Sun. A lunar spiral is representative of the Goddess as Moon Goddess, or Arcane Wisdom. By combining the spiral and the cross in a circle, you symbolize the God and the Goddess together.

Oils are applied in accordance with the purpose. They are dabbed ritually to the forehead and to the areas of the five-fold or seven-fold blessings (text page 82, and 143 for the Green Witchcraft version). They are sprinkled or dabbed on objects, around sacred spaces, and in magical receptacles and containers. For astral projection, oils are touched to the temples at either side of the head, the center of the forehead, the hollow of the throat, the pulse points at the wrists and at the inner elbows, the hollow of the palms, the back of the knees, the inside of the ankles, and the soles of the feet under the arches. In the case of astral projection, you may also want to enhance the mood by burning an incense such as jasmine, sandalwood, or benzoin.

Basic Candle Magics

Preparation of Candle

Doing spells with candles is one of the most common and effective magical practices. Once again, you will be outlining just what it is you want to do. You need to determine the focus of the spell for which the candle will be used, then look over the list of correspondences and choose the candle color (and even its scent since there are a lot of deliciously scented candles available) to match the focus. Decide what time of day and moon phase you want to use.

Select from your lists an appropriate oil with which to dress the candle, then choose the herbs you will use to enhance the power of the candle. Look over your list of runic symbols if you want to include these, and find which ones you want to inscribe on the candle. All this activity takes place as part of your outlining of your spell. You will want to have all the necessary ingredients together before you start the spell, and you may want to write out on a notecard or in your Spellbook what you are going to be doing, step by step. Here, too, you would include any timing considerations. Check the spells described on text pages 133–138 to see how they are centered around candles.

The list of symbols (text pages 105–108) will be used at the end of the spell to see what the outcome is likely to be. In other words, the wax may tell you when to expect the results to appear or how the spell will manifest. Often the symbols will simply verify to you that the spell has been effective. Not all symbols are according to the listing. You have to use your intuitive powers to interpret the images in the wax, and that is what makes witchcraft an art. Do not feel restricted to the meanings in any list of symbols if your instinct is telling you something else.

Working the Candle

Once you have drawn your circle, made your invocations, and are ready to begin your spell, rub the candle with the oil(s) you have chosen to "dress" the candle. Some people feel that only the utility knife—the bolline—should be used for inscribing a candle, others like to use the athame, or ritual knife. I feel that the energy of the charged athame is more enhancing to spellwork than the bolline I use to cut herbs, willow branches, and so forth. Inscribing a candle for magical use is not the same to me as etching symbols into a tool such as the wand, so I use the athame for candle markings.

The symbols you draw into the candle can be placed around the candle side and if the candle is wide enough, on the top around the wick. You can use your own designs, runes, ogham markings, or any of the many "witch alphabets" such as shown in *Buckland's Complete Book of Witchcraft*, by Raymond Buckland. The symbols used can be relevant to a magical focus (feoh for wealth; sigel for achievement; and wynn for joy) or you can actually spell out the purpose of the candle spell (Bring Me Money).

Now you have to focus on the desired effect, through visualization of that effect taking place, while working the candle. See the power going into the candle as you put on the oil, see the effect occuring as you inscribe the candle, and by the end of the spell, you will envision the effect as done.

Spellwork with candles is enhanced with herbs chosen to fit the purpose. Drop the selected herbs into the lighted candle, one at a time, stating the herb and the power you want drawn from the herb to work in the candle spell. You may have written a chant or a rhyme to speak as each item is added, or you may simply state something like, "basil for wealth, mint for money and blessing."

As you add herbs to the flame, feel the herbal energies moving into the spell. See the energies build in power, which you can aid at this point with dance, chant, and gesture, and when you feel the energy level is at the highest you can tolerate, release the energies by directing them to their purpose. Remember what I said earlier about using a short phrase or key word to send The Power out to complete the spell. As soon as you send that energy to complete the task, see the spell as completed and the desired effect as attained.

Let your candle burn for an hour on the altar. That is all that is needed. You can finish with whatever ritual you are doing, such as an Esbat, have your refreshment, earth the excess energy, open your circle, and put away your tools, except for the candle on the altar. After an hour, or longer if you feel the need, you may snuff out the candle and watch the cooling wax for images. Record what you saw, you could draw a little sketch for later reference, then dispose of the used candle by burying it in earth or tossing it into moving water.

Although any candle used in a spell will be disposed of after the spell is concluded, some candles may be kept and relit if dedicated to a purpose that can be renewed from time to time. A "money-as-I-need-it" focused spell or a running spell for good health are examples of renewable candle spells. For these, you would want to keep the candle someplace where you can retrieve it from time to time to relight and place it on the pentacle on the altar.

If no herbs were used in the candle, and only the top was inscribed, and then melted away, you may use the candle later on in a different spell. First you would need to terminate the original function by passing the candle through the symbols of the

Elementals (salt, incense smoke, fire, and water), then further cleanse the candle under running water. Dry it off and store it for use. The important thing here is whether or not that candle will hold for you the significance of the original spell. If it does, then bury it. Only if you can disassociate the spell from the candle itself can you use a candle again for a different spell. I only mention this practice as something that is possible, in an emergency perhaps, but I don't consider it a good idea to regularly reassign the same candle to different spells. I do recommend using small votive candles for your spells because they work well, they are not a big investment, and one candle works for one spell.

Depending on the purpose of the candle, such as a vigil candle on the altar, you can cleanse and melt a collection of such candles to make new candles. One simple and fun candle-making method is to shape the wax with a sand-mold (see illustration, p. 213). Put sand in a box (or do this at the beach), add water to make the sand wet, and shape the sand into a mold. You might want to scoop out a hole and stick a finger in three places to make feet for a cauldron-shaped candle.

Melt the used candles in a pot you don't want to cook with anymore. Hold a wick centered over the hole (wicks can be purchased at craft and hobby shops). You can use a clothespin to grip the wick on a twig, lay the twig across the rim of the hole, and then pour the melted wax into the sand mold. Let the wax cool, pop it out of the box or ground, and you have a sand-encrusted candle shaped as you designed it. You could make a star shape, or anything else your imagination devises.

Recycle used candles by melting them down to make "new" candles. A variety of molds can be used, or you can get creative as
shown here with this star-shaped, sand-cast mold.

Assignment

This is the end of the course. Throughout, I have my students individually create some of the crafts for themselves, compose a spell for class discussion, and finally, perform a ritual from start to finish, with each student taking part in one form or another. This ritual is something like the final exam for the class, and we use the time to review areas of interest, practice divination techniques, and have a question and answer session.

Try making some of the crafts, sampling teas, and casting the different types of circles. The more you do hands-on practice, the greater your confidence, and the better your skills will become. There is more to the Craft than reading about it—you need to actually put it into practice. The purpose of witchcraft is to empower yourself so you do not need to go to someone else for the things you need in your life. The Craft is about connection and self-growth, about taking control of your destiny as best you can. With the assistance of the Elementals and the loving guidance of the God and the Goddess, you can evaluate your needs and put your developing skills into practice to achieve the things you want most in your life. Bright Blessings to you as you seek your path.

—Ann Moura (Aoumiel)

Appendix 1
Casting/Opening the Ritual Circle

Casting the Circle: The Beginning of the Ritual

1. Sweep the circle area; lay out circle and altar items; bathe and robe.

2. Light incense and altar candles.

3. Ring the bell or clap your hands three times:

   The circle is about to be cast and I freely stand within to greet my Lady and my Lord.

4. Take up the center candle and light each candle of the circle, moving north, then east, south, and west, saying:

   (N) *I call upon Light and Earth at the North to illuminate and strengthen the circle.*

   (E) *I call upon Light and Air at the East to illuminate and enliven the circle.*

   (S) *I call upon Light and Fire at the South to illuminate and warm the circle.*

(W) *I call upon Light and Water at the West to illuminate and cleanse the circle.*

5. Take the athame in hand, upraised, and begin the circle at the North and move around the circle, North to East to South to West, saying:

I draw this circle in the presence of the Goddess and the God where They may come and bless Their child (name).

Lower the athame at the North, and as you walk around the circle, envision a blue light shooting out from the point and forming the circle boundary, saying:

This is the boundary of the circle. Only love shall enter and leave.

6. Return to the altar and clap or ring the bell three times.

7. Place the point of athame in the salt:

Salt is necessary to life and purifying. I bless this salt to be used in this sacred circle in the names of the Goddess and the God (state their names).

8. Pick up the salt bowl and use the tip of athame to drop three portions of salt into the water bowl, and then set the salt bowl back in its place.

9. Stir three times with the athame:

Let the blessed salt purify this water that it may be blessed to use in this sacred circle. In the names of the Goddess and the God (state their names), *I consecrate this water.*

10. Take the salted water bowl in hand and sprinkle water from it as you move deosil around the circle (N-E-S-W-N):

I consecrate this circle in the names of the Goddess and the God (names). *The circle is conjured a circle of The Power that is purified and sealed. So Mote It Be!*

11. Return the water bowl to the altar and pick up the censer; cense the circle; return the censer to altar.

12. Take anointing oil and make a solar cross ringed by a circle on your forehead:

    I (N), *am consecrated in the names of the Goddess and the God,* (names), *in this their circle.*

    (If working with family members or a Green-focused coven, cut through the air a doorway and open it to the circle with the athame for people to enter, then close the door with the athame and seal it by drawing a pentagram in the air at the base of the door. A besom or a sword may also be used, especially if it is leaned against the doorway into a room where the circle is cast to include the entry. Each person entering the circle must say the passwords, such as: "In perfect love and perfect trust" as they enter. The one who cast the circle anoints each person on the forehead with oil, drawing a symbol with the forefinger, and saying "Merry Meet." The symbol may be a solar cross, a pentagram, a spiral, a circle, a triangle, or any combination thereof, or something symbolic to your group. While this example is for Solitary use, it may be altered for family or coven participation.

13. Take the wand and hold it aloft, with both arms upraised, at North of the circle (envision a powerful bull arriving there):

    I call upon you, Elemental Earth, to attend this rite and guard this circle, for as I have body and strength, we are kith and kin!

14. Lower the wand and move to the East, raise up the wand (see devas, Fairies, or an eagle in flight):

    I call upon you, Elemental Air, to attend this rite and guard this circle, for as I breathe and think, we are kith and kin!

15. Lower the wand and move to the South, raise up the wand (see a lion or a dragon):

I call upon you, Elemental Fire, to attend this rite and guard this circle, for as I consume life to live, we are kith and kin!

16. Lower the wand and move to the West, hold the wand aloft (see an undine, a sea serpent, or a dolphin):

I call upon you, Elemental Water, to attend this rite and guard this circle, for as I feel and my heart beats, we are kith and kin!

17. Return to the altar and use the wand to draw in the air above the altar, the symbol of infinity (an 8 laying on its side)—the sign of working between the worlds.

18. Set the wand on the altar and raise up the athame in both hands overhead:

Hail to the Elementals at the Quarters! Welcome Lady and Lord to this rite! I stand between the worlds with Thy love and the Power all around!

19. Set down the athame and pick up the goblet of wine. Pour a little into the cauldron (this is a libation to the Divine in which they are honored by offering to them the first draught, then you take a sip. You may prefer to have a bowl specifically for the libation.)

20. Clap your hands or ring the bell three times.

Insert Here the Essential Ritual

(Esbats: see *Green Witchcraft*, pages 169–181)

(Sabbats: see *Green Witchcraft*, pages 183–254)

(Dark Moon Esbat: see *Green Witchcraft II*, chapter 2)

(Sidhe Moon Esbat: see *Green Witchcraft II*, chapter 4)

Appendix 1

Opening the Circle: The Closing of the Ritual

1. Ring the bell or clap your hands three times.

2. With feet spread and arms upraised:

   I acknowledge my needs and offer my appreciation to that which sustains me! May I ever remember the blessings of my Lady and my Lord.

3. With feet together, take up goblet in left hand and athame in right.

4. Slowly lower the point of the athame into the wine or other beverage:

   As male joins female for the benefit of both, let the fruits of the Divine Union promote life. Let the Earth be fruitful and let her wealth be spread throughout all lands.

5. Lay down the athame and drink from the goblet.

6. Replace the goblet on the altar and pick up the athame.

7. Touch the point of the athame to the cake in the offering dish:

   This food is the blessing of the Lady and the Lord given freely to me. As freely as I have received, may I also give food for the body, mind, and spirit to those who seek such of me.

8. Eat the Sabbat, Esbat, or other ritual food and finish the wine or other beverage:

   As I enjoy these gifts of the Goddess and the God, (names), *may I remember that without Them I would have nothing. So Mote It Be!*

9. When all is finished, hold the athame in your power hand, level over the altar:

Lord and Lady, I am blessed by your sharing this time with me; watching and guarding me, and guiding me here and in all things. I came in love and I depart in love.

10. Raise up the athame in a salute:

Love is the Law and Love is the Bond. Merry did I meet, merry do I part, and merry will I meet again. Merry meet, merry part, and merry meet again! The circle is now cleared. So Mote It Be!

11. Kiss the flat of the blade and set the athame on the altar.

12. Take up the snuffer, go to the North, and raise up your open arms:

Depart in peace, Elemental Earth. (At this point in each farewell, you may want to add your own sentiments of kinship and appreciation.) *My blessings take with you!* (Lower arms and snuff the candle; envision the Elemental Power departing.)

13. Go to the East, raise up your arms:

Depart in peace, Elemental Air. My blessings take with you! (Lower your arms and snuff out the candle; envision the Elemental Power departing.)

14. Go to the South, raise up your arms:

Depart in peace, Elemental Fire. My blessings take with you! (Lower arms and snuff the candle; envision the Elemental Power departing.)

15. Go to the West, raise up your arms:

Depart in peace, Elemental Water. My blessings take with you! (Lower your arms and snuff out the candle; envision the Elemental Power departing.)

16. Return to the altar and set down the snuffer. Raise up your arms:

Beings and powers of the visible and invisible, depart in peace! You aid in my work, whisper in my mind, and bless me from other worlds. Let there always be harmony between us. My blessings take with you. The circle is cleared.

17. Take up the athame, go to the North, point the athame down and move widdershins (counterclockwise) around the circle (N-W-S-E-N), envisioning the blue light drawing back into the athame:

The circle is open, yet the circle remains as its magical power is drawn back into me. (When you return to the North, having walked the circle, raise up the athame so the blade touches your forehead, and envision the blue light swirling around back into you.)

18. Return to the altar:

The ceremony is ended. Blessings have been given and blessings have been received, may the peace of the Goddess and the God remain in my heart. So Mote It Be!

19. Set down the athame. Put away all the magical tools and clear the altar.

20. The cauldron or libation bowl contents are poured onto the earth (either outdoors or in a potted plant, or into the sink under running water).

Appendix 2
Mail Order Supplies

ABYSS DISTRIBUTION
  48 Chester Road
  Chester, MA 01011-9735
  (413) 623-2155
  email: AbyssDist@aol.com

AVALON
  1211 Hillcrest Street
  Orlando, FL 32803
  (407) 895-7439

EYE OF THE CAT
  3314 E. Broadway
  Long Beach, CA 90803
  (310) 438-3569

EYE OF THE DAY
  P.O. Box 21261
  Boulder, CO 80308
  1-800-717-3307

JBL STATUES
P.O. Box 163
Crozet, VA 22932
http://www.jblstatue.com

LUNATRIX
P.O. Box 800482
Santa Clarita, CA 91380-0482

MAGIC BOOK STORE
2306 Highland AveNUE
National City, CA 91950
(619) 477-5260

ROOTS AND WINGS
16607 Barberry – C2
Southgate, MI 48195
(313) 285-3679

WHITE LIGHT PENTACLES/
SACRED SPIRIT PRODUCTS
P.O. Box 8163
Salem, MA 01971-8163

WORLDWIDE CURIO HOUSE
P.O. Box 17095
Minneapolis, MN 55417

Glossary

Animistic: seeing all things as having an "anima" or "soul," a bit of the spirit of the Divine or the Power in everything.

Athame (a'tha-may or a-thaw'may): ritual knife of witchcraft used to direct energy in magical work; generally a black-handled knife, but any knife or knife-like object used to conduct energy for magic work may be an athame.

Black Mirror: tool used for divination and dark aspect meditations.

Bodily Energy Points: base of spine, abdomen, stomach, heart, throat, forehead, crown (top) of head.

Bolline (bo-leen'): practical knife of witchcraft used to cut with and inscribe objects; generally a white or brown-handled knife, but some witches may utilize only one knife for the work of both the athame and bolline.

Casting Cloth: the designed cloth laid out for a divination throw, usually for ogham, although sometimes used for runes or tarot.

Celts: Indo-Europeans who arrived in Ireland by way of Spain; people originally of Dravidic derivation from the Indus Valley.

Ceremonial Magic: magic system based on the Hebrew Kabbalah of twelfth-century Europe.

Charms: objects made and infused with magical energy and carried or placed to achieve a goal (such as protection).

Circle: ritual area created to contain raised energy that may be directed in spell work.

Coven: assembly of witchcraft practitioners, generally adhering to the standardized procedures of a particular Tradition or those agreed upon by the membership, usually twelve in number, with one Priest or Priestess to make a total of thirteen members, although there may be two leaders, male and female.

Craft: witchcraft, the Old Religion.

Deflection Magic: defuse general malevolence and ill will of others.

Dressing: putting an oil on spell items such as candles as part of a ritual consecration to prepare the object to attract and direct the energy of a spell to accomplish a goal.

Elemental Energy Points: palms of the hands and soles of the feet; right hand is Fire, left hand is Water, left foot is Earth, and right foot is Air.

Esbat (Es'bat): lunar celebrations of witches during the Full and New Moons; often used in conjunction with spellwork.

Exorcism: aid spirits in passage; disperse negative energies to allow positive energies to enter.

Familiar: witch's animal or spirit helper in magical work.

Frey: "Lord"; Vanir God of Green level of Teutonic system, God of the World, animals, land, fertility, eroticism, peace and well-being, twin of Freya.

Freya: "Lady"; Vanir Goddess of Green level of Teutonic system who is able to travel to the levels of law and creation; Goddess of magic, cycles of nature, taught Odin magic, twin of Frey.

Generator: large crystal used to charge other crystals.

Grimoires: books of ceremonial magicians dating from twelfth-to sixteenth-century Europe containing elaborate rituals, names of power, making of magical seals, and lists of correspondences.

Hallowed: holy.

Hallows: sacred, holy, consecrated; a time when the veil between the worlds is thin and there is easy passage, hence the holy time of Hallow'een (Samhain).

Holey Stone: symbol of the regenerative power of the Goddess; yoni.

Inhabited: companion or other spirit entity dwelling in a crystal from time to time. It may be contacted through that crystal.

Ken (Kenning): all-encompassing sensation of "knowing" something with a certitude and acceptance that what is kenned, *is*; keen, instinctive insight.

List of Correspondences: magical function and description of items used in the practice of the Craft.

Linga: phallic symbol of creative powers of the God.

Lord and Lady: the God and the Goddess of the Old Religion, deities of nature and the universe through whom the Power flows.

Magic: creating changes by the gathering, focusing, and directing of energy.

Mannuz (Ma-nu'): the Self as part of the Universe and the Divine.

Meditation: relaxing to open an altered state of awareness in which the conscious mind is subdued to let the subconscious mind functions dominate; state of relaxation and accessibility.

Names of Power: names chanted for power-raising; can be derived from Grimoires, with many being ancient deity names redefined as demons or spirits.

Ogham: old Celtic alphabet symbols named for trees and used for magical symbolism.

Old Religion: pre-Christian nature religions of Europe.

Pagan: *country*; religion of the country folk who retained the traditions of the Old Religion during the Christianization of Europe; modern name used for all non-Christian religions.

Power Hand: the hand a person favors, used in ritual context for the power found in the dominant hand.

The Power: the universal life-energies of the Divine expressed through the Elementals, the Deities, and such cosmic bodies as the Sun, the Moon, the Earth, planets, stars, comets, and meteors.

Rituals: magical or devotional ceremonies in which energy is raised and the practitioner is united with the Divine in religious observances, meditative states, or for the conducting of magic as with spell work.

Runes: old Teutonic and Norse alphabet symbols associated with magical meanings.

Sabbat (Sab'bat'): the eight holy days of witchcraft and Wicca representing the solstices, equinoxes, planting and harvest cycles; often the Sabbats are reversed for the Southern Hemisphere to align with seasonal changes, although some practitioners prefer to celebrate according to the traditional European dates.

Spells: magic gathered and directed in ritual to achieve a goal.

Symbols: letters and designs used in Craft work and spells.

Symbolism: meanings and interpretations for divination images and omens.

Tarot (Tair'roe): cards descended from India, modern deck of seventy-eight cards, originally used in a game called *Tarrochi* in the fifteenth century, now used mainly in divination; the deck contains twenty-one archetype cards called the Major Arcana, and those typical of regular playing cards, called the

Minor Arcana, with the addition of a page or princess card for each suit.

Traditions: witchcraft or Wiccan denominations dating from the 1940s through the 1990s, with many requiring a chain of denominational initiation based on Tradition instruction.

Turning of the wheel: passage thru the yearly cycle of eight Sabbats; hence, the passage of the year marked by the celebrations therein.

Yoni: vagina, or womb; round stone with a central hole is a Goddess symbol for giving birth to all life.

Witchcraft. the *Craft of the Wise,* Nature-based magical religion and practice; the Old Religion of pagan Europe.

Selected
Bibliography

Adler, Margot. *Drawing Down the Moon; Witches, Druids, Goddess-Worshippers, and Other Pagans in America Today.* Boston: Beacon Press, 1979.

Aoumiel. *Dancing Shadows: The Roots of Western Religious Beliefs.* St. Paul: Llewellyn Publications, 1991.

Baring, Anne and Cashford, Jules. *The Myth of the Goddess.* London: Arkana Penguin Books, 1993.

Briggs, Katherine. *An Encyclopedia of Fairies, Hobgoblins, Brownies, Bogies, and Other Supernatural Creatures.* New York: Pantheon Books, 1976.

Buckland, Raymond. *Buckland's Complete Book of Witchcraft.* St. Paul: Llewellyn Worldwide, 1986.

Campbell, Joseph. *The Masks of God: Oriental Mythology.* New York: Penguin Books, 1976.

———. *The Masks of God: Primitive Mythology.* New York: Penguin Books, 1976.

Carlyon, Richard. *A Guide to the Gods.* New York: Quill, William Morrow, 1981.

Cavendish, Richard. *The Black Arts.* New York: Perigee Books, The Berkeley Publishing Group, 1967.

Conway, D. J. *Celtic Magic*. St. Paul: Llewellyn Publications, 1990.

Cunliffe, Barry. *The Celtic World*. New York: Greenwich House, Crown Publishers, Inc. 1986.

Cunningham, Scott. *The Complete Book of Incense, Oils, & Brews*. St. Paul: Llewellyn Publications, 1990.

Durant, Will. *The Story of Civilization: Part I: Our Oriental Heritage*. New York: Simon and Schuster, 1954.

———. *The Story of Civilization: Part II: The Life of Greece*. New York: Simon and Schuster, 1966.

———. *The Story of Civilization: Part IV: The Age of Faith*. New York: Simon and Schuster, 1950.

Eliot, Alexander. *The Universal Myths: Heroes, Gods, Tricksters and Others*. New York: Meridian Books, 1990.

Evans-Wentz, W. Y. *The Fairy-Faith in Celtic Countries*. New York: Carol Publishing Group, 1994.

Francisis, Alfonso de. *Pompeii*. Napoli, Italy: Interdipress, 1972.

Gimbutas, Marija. *The Civilization of the Goddess, the World of Old Europe*. Edited by Joan Marler. San Francisco: HarperCollins Publishers, 1991.

González-Wippler, Migene. *The Complete Book of Spells, Ceremonies & Magic*. St. Paul: Llewellyn Publications, 1988.

Goodrich, Norma Lorre. *Priestesses*. New York: Harper Perennial, 1989.

Graves, Robert. *The White Goddess, a Historical Grammar of Poetic Myth*. New York: The Noonday Press, Farrar, Straus and Giroux, amended and enlarged edition, 1966.

Green, Marian. *A Witch Alone*. London: The Aquarian Press, 1991.

Kramker, S. N. *The Sumerians, Their History, Culture, and Character*. Chicago: University of Chicago Press, 1963.

Llewellyn. *Llewellyn's 1998 Magical Almanac*. St. Paul: Llewellyn Worldwide, 1997.

Massa, Aldo. *The World of the Etruscans*. Translated by John Christmas. Geneve, Italy: Minerva, 1989.

Moura, Ann (Aoumiel). *Green Witchcraft: Folk Magic, Fairy Lore & Herb Craft*. St. Paul: Llewellyn Publications, 1996.

———. *Green Witchcraft II: Balancing Light and Shadow*. St. Paul: Llewellyn Publications, 1998.

Scott, Michael. *Irish Folk & Fairytale Omnibus*. UK: Sphere Books Ltd., 1983, 1984; New York: Barnes & Noble Books, 1983.

Sjoo, Monica and Mor, Barbara. *The Great Cosmic Mother*. San Francisco: HarperCollins Publishers, 1991.

Squire, Charles. *Celtic Myth and Legend*. Newcastle: Newcastle Publishing Co., Inc., 1975.

Starhawk. *The Spiral Dance: A Rebirth of the Ancient Religion of the Great Goddess*. New York: HarperCollins Publishers, 1989.

Stone, Merlin. *When God was a Woman*. New York: Dorset Press, 1976.

Taylour, Lord William. *The Mycenaeans*. London: Thames and Hudson Ltd., 1994.

Thorsson, Edred. *The Book of Ogham: The Celtic Tree Oracle*. St. Paul: Llewellyn Publications, 1994.

———. *Northern Magic; Mysteries of the Norse, Germans & English*. St. Paul: Llewellyn Publications, 1992.

Walker, Barbara G., *The Crone, Woman of Age, Wisdom, and Power*. San Francisco: HarperCollins Publishers, 1985.

Woolley, C. Leonard. *The Sumerians*. New York: W. W. Norton & Company, 1965.

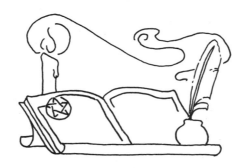

Index

☽ REACH FOR THE MOON

Llewellyn publishes hundreds of books on your favorite subjects! To get these exciting books, including the ones on the following pages, check your local bookstore or order them directly from Llewellyn.

ORDER BY PHONE

- Call toll-free within the U.S. and Canada, 1-800-THE MOON
- In Minnesota, call (651) 291-1970
- We accept VISA, MasterCard, and American Express

ORDER BY MAIL

- Send the full price of your order (MN residents add 7% sales tax) in U.S. funds, plus postage & handling to:

  Llewellyn Worldwide
  P.O. Box 64383, Dept. K688–2
  St. Paul, MN 55164–0383, U.S.A.

POSTAGE & HANDLING

(For the U.S., Canada, and Mexico)

- $4.00 for orders $15.00 and under
- $5.00 for orders over $15.00
- No charge for orders over $100.00

We ship UPS in the continental United States. We ship standard mail to P.O. boxes. Orders shipped to Alaska, Hawaii, The Virgin Islands, and Puerto Rico are sent first-class mail. Orders shipped to Canada and Mexico are sent surface mail.

International orders: Airmail—add freight equal to price of each book to the total price of order, plus $5.00 for each non-book item (audio tapes, etc.).

Surface mail—Add $1.00 per item.

Allow 2 weeks for delivery on all orders.
Postage and handling rates subject to change.

DISCOUNTS

We offer a 20% discount to group leaders or agents. You must order a minimum of 5 copies of the same book to get our special quantity price.

FREE CATALOG

Get a free copy of our color catalog, *New Worlds of Mind and Spirit*. Subscribe for just $10.00 in the United States and Canada ($30.00 overseas, airmail). Many bookstores carry *New Worlds*—ask for it!

Visit our web site at www.llewellyn.com for more information.

GREEN WITCHCRAFT
Folk Magic, Fairy Lore
& Herb Craft

Ann Moura (Aoumiel)

Very little has been written about traditional family practices of the Old Religion
simply because such information has not
been offered for popular consumption. If
you have no contacts with these traditions,
Green Witchcraft will meet your need for a
practice based in family and natural Witchcraft traditions.

Green Witchcraft describes the worship of nature and the use of herbs
that have been part of human culture from the earliest times. It relates to
the Lord and Lady of Greenwood, the Primal Father and Mother, and to
the Earth Spirits called Faeries.

Green Witchcraft traces the historic and folk background of this path
and teaches its practical techniques. Learn the basics of Witchcraft from
a third-generation, traditional family Green Witch who openly shares
from her own experiences. Through a how-to format you'll learn rites of
passage, activities for Sabbats and Esbats, Fairy lore, self-dedication, self-
initiation, spellwork, herbcraft and divination.

This practical handbook is an invitation to explore, identify and adapt
the Green elements of Witchcraft that work for you, today.

1-56718-690-4, 288 pp., 6 x 9, illus.   **$14.95**

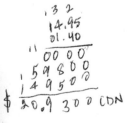

TO ORDER, CALL 1-800-THE MOON
Prices subject to change without notice.

GREEN WITCHCRAFT II
Balancing Light & Shadow

Ann Moura (Aoumiel)

The Green Witch is a natural witch, a cottage witch, and a solitary witch. This witch does not fear nature and the woods, but finds a sense of belonging and connection with the earth and the universe. Now, in this sequel to *Green Witchcraft*, hereditary witch Ann Moura dispels the common misunderstandings and prejudices against the "shadow side" of nature, the self, and the Divine. She presents a practical guide on how to access and utilize the dark powers in conjunction with the light to achieve a balanced magical practice and move towards spiritual wholeness.

Guided meditations, step-by-step rituals, and spells enable you to connect with the dark powers, invoke their energies, and achieve your goals through magical workings. Face your greatest fears so you can release them, create an elemental bottle to attract faery life, burn herbs to open your subconscious awareness, learn to use the ogham for travel to other worlds, recognize and name a familiar, and much more.

ISBN: 1-56718-689-0, 288 pp., 6 x 9, illus. $12.95

$ 18.95

TO ORDER, CALL 1-800-THE MOON
Prices subject to change without notice.

INSIDE A WITCHES' COVEN

Edain McCoy

Inside a Witches' Coven gives you an insider's look at how a real Witches' coven operates, from initiation and secret vows to parting rituals. You'll get step-by-step guidance for joining or forming a coven, plus sage advice and exclusive insights to help you decide which group is the right one for you.

Maybe you're thinking about joining a coven, but don't know what to expect, or how to make contacts. Perhaps you already belong to a coven, but your group needs ideas for organizing a teaching circle or mediating conflicts. Either way, you're sure to find *Inside a Witches' Coven* a practical source of wisdom.

Joining a coven can be an important step in your spiritual life. Before you take that step, let a practicing Witch lead you through the hidden inner workings of a Witches' coven.

1-56718-666-1, 224 pp., 5.25 x 8   **$9.95**

TO ORDER, CALL 1-800-THE MOON
Prices subject to change without notice.

WICCA
A Guide for the Solitary Practitioner
Scott Cunningham

Wicca is a book of life, and how to live magically, spiritually, and wholly attuned with Nature. It is a book of sense and common sense, not only about Magick, but about religion and one of the most critical issues of today: how to achieve the much needed and wholesome relationship with our Earth. Cunningham presents Wicca as it is today: a gentle, Earth-oriented religion dedicated to the Goddess and God. This book fulfills a need for a practical guide to solitary Wicca—a need which no previous book has fulfilled.

Here is a positive, practical introduction to the religion of Wicca, designed so that any interested person can learn to practice the religion alone, anywhere in the world. It presents Wicca honestly and clearly, without the pseudo-history that permeates other books. It shows that Wicca is a vital, satisfying part of twentieth century life.

This book presents the theory and practice of Wicca from an individual's perspective. The section on the Standing Stones Book of Shadows contains solitary rituals for the Esbats and Sabbats. This book, based on the author's nearly two decades of Wiccan practice, presents an eclectic picture of various aspects of this religion. Exercises designed to develop magical proficiency, a self-dedication ritual, herb, crystal and rune magic, as well as recipes for Sabbat feasts, are included in this excellent book.

0-87542-118-0, 240 pp., 6 x 9, illus.   **$9.95**

TO ORDER, CALL 1-800-THE MOON
Prices subject to change without notice.

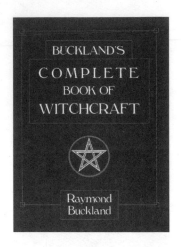

BUCKLAND'S COMPLETE BOOK OF WITCHCRAFT

Raymond Buckland

Here is the most complete resource to the study and practice of modern, non-denominational Wicca. This is a lavishly illustrated, self-study course for the solitary or group. Included are rituals; exercises for developing psychic talents; information on all major "sects" of the Craft; sections on tools, beliefs, dreams, meditations, divination, herbal lore, healing, ritual clothing and much, much more. This book unites theory and practice into a comprehensive course designed to help you develop into a practicing Witch, one of the "Wise Ones." It is written by Ray Buckland, a very famous and respected authority on Witchcraft who first came public with the Old Religion in the United States. Large format with workbook-type exercises, profusely illustrated and full of music and chants. Takes you from A to Z in the study of Witchcraft.

Never before has so much information on the Craft of the Wise been collected in one place. Traditionally, there are three degrees of advancement in most Wiccan traditions. When you have completed studying this book, you will be the equivalent of a Third-Degree Witch. Even those who have practiced Wicca for years find useful information in this book, and many covens are using this for their textbook. If you want to become a Witch, or if you merely want to find out what Witchcraft is really about, you will find no better book than this.

0-87542-050-8, 272 pp., 8.5 x 11, illus. **$16.95**

TO ORDER, CALL 1-800-THE MOON
Prices subject to change without notice.

TO STIR A MAGICK CAULDRON
A Witch's Guide to Casting and Conjuring

Silver RavenWolf

The sequel to the enormously popular *To Ride a Silver Broomstick: New Generation Witchcraft*. This upbeat and down-to-earth guide to intermediate-level witchery was written for all Witches—solitaries, eclectics, and traditionalists. In her warm, straight-from-the-hip, eminently knowledgeable manner, Silver provides explanations, techniques, exercises, anecdotes, and guidance on traditional and modern aspects of the Craft, both as a science and as a religion.

Find out why you should practice daily devotions and how to create a sacred space. Learn six ways to cast a magick circle. Explore the complete art of spell-casting. Examine the hows and whys of Craft laws, oaths, degrees, lineage, traditions, and more. Explore the ten paths of power, and harness this wisdom for your own spell-craft. This book offers you dozens of techniques—some never before published—to help you uncover the benefits of natural magick and ritual and make them work for you—without spending a dime!

Silver is a "working Witch" who has successfully used each and every technique and spell in this book. By the time you have done the exercises in each chapter, you will be well-trained in the first level of initiate studies. Test your knowledge with the Wicca 101 test provided at the back of the book and become a certified Witch! Learn to live life to its fullest through this positive spiritual path.

1-56718-424-3, 320 pp., 7 x 10, illus.   **$14.95**

TO ORDER, CALL 1-800-THE MOON
Prices subject to change without notice.

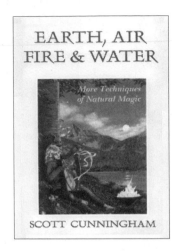

EARTH, AIR, FIRE & WATER
More Techniques of Natural Magic

Scott Cunningham

A water-smoothed stone . . . The wind . . . A candle's flame . . . A pool of water. These are the age-old tools of natural magic. Born of the Earth, possessing inner power, they await only our touch and intention to bring them to life.

The four Elements are the ancient powerhouses of magic. Using their energies, we can transform ourselves, our lives and our worlds. Tap into the marvelous powers of the natural world with these rites, spells and simple rituals that you can do easily and with a minimum of equipment. *Earth, Air, Fire & Water* includes more than 75 spells, rituals and ceremonies with detailed instructions for designing your own magical spells. This book instills a sense of wonder concerning our planet and our lives; and promotes a natural, positive practice that anyone can successfully perform.

0-897542-131-8, 240 pp., 6 x 9, illus. **$9.95**

TO ORDER, CALL 1-800-THE MOON
Prices subject to change without notice.

EMBRACING THE MOON
A Witch's Guide to Rituals, Spellcraft & Shadow Work

Yasmine Galenorn

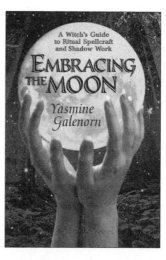

Do you feel like toasting the Gods with a glass of mead as you revel in the joys of life? Ever wish you could creep through the mists at night, hunting the Wild Lord? *Embracing the Moon* takes you into the core of Witchcraft, helping you weave magic into your daily routine. The spells and rituals are designed to give you the flexibility to experiment so that you are not locked into dogmatic, rigid degree-systems. Written to encompass both beginning and advanced practitioners, Embracing the Moon explores the mystical side of natural magic while keeping a common-sense attitude.

Packed not only with spells and rituals, but recipes for oils, spell powders and charms, this book is based on personal experience; the author dots the pages with her own stories and anecdotes to give you fascinating, and sometimes humorous, examples of what you might expect out of working with her system of magic.

1-56718-304-2, 312 pp., 6 x 9, illus.   **$14.95**

TO ORDER, CALL 1-800-THE MOON
Prices subject to change without notice.

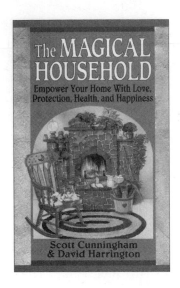

THE MAGICAL HOUSEHOLD
Empower Your Home with Love, Protection, Health and Happiness

Scott Cunningham & David Harrington

Whether your home is a small apartment or a palatial mansion, you want it to be something special. Now it can be with *The Magical Household*. Learn how to make your home more than just a place to live. Turn it into a place of security, life, fun and magic. Here you will not find the complex magic of the ceremonial magician. Rather, you will learn simple, quick and effective magical spells that use nothing more than common items in your house: furniture, windows, doors, carpet, pets, etc. You will learn to take advantage of the intrinsic power and energy that is already in your home, waiting to be tapped. You will learn to make magic a part of your life. The result is a home that is safeguarded from harm and a place which will bring you happiness, health and more.

0-87542-124-5, 208 pp., 5.25 x 8, illus.   **$9.95**

TO ORDER, CALL 1-800-THE MOON
Prices subject to change without notice.

THE FAMILY WICCA BOOK
The Craft for Parents & Children
Ashleen O'Gaea

Enjoy the first book written for Pagan parents! The number of Witches raising children to the Craft is growing. The need for mutual support is rising—yet until now, there have been no books that speak to a Wiccan family's needs and experience. Finally, here is *The Family Wicca Book*, full to the brim with rituals, projects, encouragement and practical discussion of real-life challenges. You'll find lots of ideas to use right away.

Is magic safe for children? Why do some people think Wiccans are Satanists? How do you make friends with spirits and little people in the local woods? Find out how one Wiccan family gives clear and honest answers to questions that intrigue pagans all over the world.

When you want to ground your family in Wicca without ugly "bashing;" explain life, sex, and death without embarrassment; and add to your Sabbats without much trouble or expense, *The Family Wicca Book* is required reading. You'll refer to it again and again as your traditions grow with your family.

0-87542-591-7, 240 pgs., 5.25 x 8, illus.   **$9.95**

TO ORDER, CALL 1-800-THE MOON
Prices subject to change without notice.

PRACTICAL CANDLE-BURNING RITUALS
Spells & Rituals for Every Purpose
Raymond Buckland

Magick is a way in which to apply the full range of your hidden psychic powers to the problems we all face in daily life. We know that normally we use only five percent of our total powers. Magick taps powers from deep inside our psyche where we are in contact with the universe's limitless resources.

Magick need not be complex—it can be as simple as using a few candles to focus your mind, a simple ritual to give direction to your desire, a few words to give expression to your wish.

This book shows you how easy it can be. Here is magick for fun, magick as a craft, magick for success, love, luck, money, marriage, and healing. Practice magick to stop slander, to learn truth, to heal an unhappy marriage, to overcome a bad habit, to break up a love affair, etc.

Magick—with nothing fancier than ordinary candles, and the 28 rituals in this book (given in both Christian and Old Religion versions)—can transform your life.

0-87542-048-6, 208 pp., 5.25 x 8, illus.   **$7.95**

TO ORDER, CALL 1-800-THE MOON
Prices subject to change without notice.

SPELL CRAFTS
Creating Magical Objects

Scott Cunningham & David Harrington

Since early times, crafts have been intimately linked with spirituality. When a woman carefully shaped a water jar from the clay she'd gathered from a river bank, she was performing a spiritual practice. When crafts were used to create objects intended for ritual or that symbolized the Divine, the connection between the craftsperson and divinity grew more intense. Today, handcrafts can still be more than a pastime—they can be rites of power and honor; a religious ritual. After all, hands were our first magical tools.

Spell Crafts is a modern guide to creating physical objects for the attainment of specific magical goals. It is far different from magic books that explain how to use purchased magical tools. You will learn how to fashion spell brooms, weave wheat, dip candles, sculpt clay, mix herbs, bead sacred symbols and much more, for a variety of purposes. Whatever your craft, you will experience the natural process of moving energy from within yourself (or within natural objects) to create positive change.

0-87542-185-7, 224 pp., 5.25 x 8, illus., photos **$10.00**

TO ORDER, CALL 1-800-THE MOON
Prices subject to change without notice.